THE "REAL HOUSEWIFE" SWINDLER

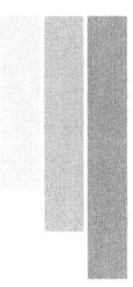

THE "REAL HOUSEWIFE" SWINDLER

BRIDGET R. KNIGHT

Copyright © 2023 by Bridget R. Knight

All rights reserved. No part of this publication may be reproduced or transmitted in any form or by any means electronic or mechanical, including photography, recording, or any information storage and retrieval system now known or to be invented, without permission in writing from the publisher, except by a reviewer who wishes to quote brief passages in connection with a review written for inclusion in a magazine, newspaper, website, or broadcast.

For privacy reasons, some names, locations, and dates may have been changed.

ISBN: 9798390378090 (Paperback)
ISBN: 978-0-000000-0 (Hardcover)

Library of Congress Control Number: 00000000000

Book design by
Manufactured in the United States of America
First printing edition 2023.

CONTENTS

Introduction	ix
Chapter One THE CALM DURING THE GRIFT	1
The Four Expectations	3
Getting Down to Business	5
Phase One	7
Phase Two	8
Enrollment Fees Adding Up	9
Chapter Two THE PRESSURE	17
Stress Overload	22
Back to the Grind	25
Tax Season Blues	26
Business Credit Woes	28
A Change of Scenery	29
More Letdowns	30
Chapter Three THE DEMANDS	35
The Next Con	36
Taking the Bull by the Horns	39
Another Suffered Heart Attack	46
Chapter Four THE RESOLUTION	49
Last Ditch Effort	52
Chapter Five THE REVELATION	59
Nationwide Scam Exposed	60
Next Steps	62
Chapter Six THE U.S. v. JENNIFER SHAH	65
Glorious Days Ahead	68
Chapter Seven THE PLEA DEAL	71

Chapter Eight THE LONG PAUSE	81
Chapter Nine THE SENTENCE	87
Chapter Ten THE TRUTH BEHIND THE GRIFT	95
Tricks of the Trade	97
Pulling it all Together	101
Conclusion	107
Acknowledgements	113

INTRODUCTION

A grifter has a powerful grip! I learned this the hard way, and unfortunately, I learned this lesson much too late. In October of 2017, I became a victim of a nationwide telemarketing scheme, carried out by a woman named Jennifer Shah, along with her associates. If you are familiar with or know Jennifer Shah, then you know that she is a TV celebrity on *The Real Housewives of Salt Lake City* in Utah. You may already know that she and her co-conspirators have been imprisoned or will soon be imprisoned for their participation in this telemarketing scheme. You may already know that Jennifer Shah had a way of flaunting her lavish lifestyle. You may also already know that Jennifer portrayed herself as a wealthy and successful businesswoman, bragging about earning millions of dollars. But what you may not know is how sophisticated her con game was and how deeply she was rooted in that game. You may not know how Jennifer and her associates conspired to target a certain group of individuals to pull off their con and keep it going for many, many years. You may not know how their actions caused devastation and life-changing events for the victims. You may not know the full story of how the victims were preyed upon and swindled repeatedly. This book, however, reveals the ugly truth about how Jennifer and her associates conspired to "hook" and defraud elderly victims, and how they cleverly conspired to cover it up.

More specifically, this book describes my own personal journey as a victim of Jennifer's game, from the very beginning of the con to the end. It uncovers the shocking truth about how Jennifer and her associates used well-established "tricks of the trade" to swindle victims over the age of fifty-five, including myself, out of tens of thousands of dollars. Once I was HOOKED, it was nearly impossible for me to break free. It started off as a simple investment but quickly spiraled out-of-control. Jennifer and her associates managed to drain my pocketbook, little-by-little with the promise of a profitable online home-based business. The scam involved many players, all operating from the same playbook. Sadly, the scam also involved thousands of elderly victims who ended up losing their livelihood.

Once I realized that I was being scammed, I immediately wanted OUT. Unfortunately, breaking free from this hellhole resulted in dire consequences for me, health-wise. Yet, I had no other recourse. I did what I needed to do. I fought hard to recover my money and to put this tragic part of my life behind me. I wanted to escape and forget this ever happened. It would be years later when I found myself involved in the Jennifer Shah saga all over again, but this time the game changed. It began with a phone call from Homeland Security Investigations in March of 2021. This phone call was definitely life-changing for me, but in a good way. Jennifer Shah's empire had imploded! Now, it was my turn to fight back and assist the prosecution with their case against Jennifer. I swung into action quickly.

It would take several more months before learning about the criminal charges that Jennifer Shah and her co-conspirators were facing or had already faced. Likewise, it would be a few more months before learning about their outcomes, pleas, and prison sentences. It all started to unfold little-by-little. At the time of writing of this book, I continue to learn the fate of each one of Jennifer's accomplices. They all deserved what they got.

The difference between a grifter and a thief is that a grifter tricks you out of money through lies, and a thief takes your money by force. In most cases, you can see a thief coming. You can't spot a grifter until they've got you in their powerful grip. The grift is real and it will consume anyone who is not "woke" or paying close attention to the red flags. Anyone can become a victim of fraud; young or old, black or white, rich or poor, regardless of one's educational or career status. Grifters do not discriminate, but we can thwart their attempts. This book provides some insight into how con artists think, operate, and how they prey on their victims. Grifters count on us to be an easy prey. They all operate from basically the same playbook and will stop at nothing to hook you and reel you in. This book also provides some insight on how to recognize a scam to avoid becoming a victim, and what to do if you, unfortunately, do become a victim of a scam. Sometimes, however, it is not easy protecting oneself from con artists because they are sly and masters at their game. Still, once we have been scammed, we have to do everything that's humanly possible to not fall prey to another scam.

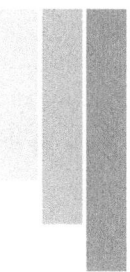

CHAPTER ONE
THE CALM DURING THE GRIFT

I never saw it coming. I guess this is what a lot of people say once they discover that they are a victim of a con. I imagine that the next thing that goes through their mind is, "How did I allow this to happen?" A *grifter* has a powerful grip. They will instantly take hold of you and they won't let go. Vulnerability soon sets in. All reasoning and understanding go right out the window. Your brain becomes scrambled. From the very beginning, you want to believe that what you're about to embark on or invest in is legitimate. You want to believe that what the other person is proclaiming is honest and truthful. You want to believe that the product the other person is selling is *real*. You want to believe that the voice on the other end of the phone is genuine. Sadly, this is not always the case. Mid-October of 2017 marked the beginning of the grift. I never saw it coming. My life was forever changed, and not in a good way. It all started with two phone calls; calls that I never should have taken. My first instinct was to just ignore the calls because it was the end

1

of a long workday. I was preparing to pack up my bags, silence my cell phone, and head directly home. Unfortunately, I didn't follow my gut instinct. A part of me was curious because during the early part of October, I had completed a number of job searches online. I was ready for a career change and was seeking that perfect, or near perfect, niche. Being a widow with just one source of income had its challenges. My beautiful husband of twelve years passed away in June of 2015 from a year-long bout with cancer. Shortly after his cancer diagnosis, he was declared disabled and started receiving Social Security disability benefits each month up until his death. So, just like that, the benefits stopped.

I had worked in the field of education, both as a licensed teacher and school administrator, since 1986 and was burnt out. I wanted so badly to retire early from my job as a teacher and supplement my retirement income with earnings from a new job, ideally a home-based business. I knew for sure that I would find a suitable, well-paying job that could make me happy and not burn me out. Some of the jobs that had piqued my interest during my searches online weren't necessarily home-based businesses, but they were very interesting, nonetheless. Earlier that month, I had applied for a couple of jobs that I later interviewed for, but nothing really materialized. However, at the end of my workday in mid-October, everything changed for me.

Again, I received two separate phone calls at the end of my workday from two sales representatives named Mitch and David. I didn't know it then, but this marked the beginning of a journey that started as a simple plan and ended up being a deliberate, deceitful, and well-orchestrated nationwide CON. Mitch was the first player I spoke with in Jennifer Shah's long con game, then David. David did most of the talking. They were both very smooth talkers and they told me everything that I wanted to hear about creating wealth. It wasn't merely about creating wealth, as David phrased it. Instead, it was more about, *"Creating wealth by using other people's money."* This was the hook. David used all the right words. All con artists, I suppose, have a way of hooking their prey with a clever line or famous quote. Once you're hooked, you lose all sense of reality. You become a different person, as if your DNA has undergone a complete transformation. Your thinking and reasoning become a big blur. You are no longer yourself and you're no longer able to make careful and reasonable decisions. At least, that is what happened to me. David cleverly convinced me that I could create wealth by using other people's money with affiliate marketing, and I fell for the con.

THE FOUR EXPECTATIONS

There were only four expectations needed to create this wealth, according to David, and I had to commit to all four of them. David made it seem so easy. A grifter has a powerful grip. The first expectation that David described to me was *time*. In order that I create wealth, I had to commit or devote 10-15 hours each week to my business, seven days a week. This seemed reasonable to me. There was nothing outrageous about this expectation; only 10-15 hours per week. I could do this. Once you're hooked, however, you're no longer able to think clearly and ask yourself the hard questions. Your judgement becomes cloudy. A part of you may think that it's too good to be true, but you don't listen to that little "voice of reasoning."

The second expectation was to be *teachable*. David passionately explained that I had to be a teachable person to make it in the affiliate marketing business. In other words, I had to be receptive or willing to learn all the material presented and apply myself by completing all the assignments given to me by their expert coaches. Again, this all seemed reasonable to me. I mumbled to myself, "I had always been a good student throughout elementary school, high school, and college." So, I knew that I could easily meet this expectation.

The third expectation that David described was education, investment, and the use of Capital Leverage. David went on to explain that Capital Leverage was using other people's money (e.g., the bank's money) to make money, thus creating wealth. He further explained that there were two types of debt: negative debt (e.g., car and TV purchases) and positive debt (e.g., using credit cards). He carefully delineated the differences and proclaimed that any debt that doesn't make money is considered negative debt. So, I would need to create positive debt by using my credit cards to start up my affiliate marketing home-based business. This seemed to make good sense at first. Looking back, I didn't realize how positive debt could easily lead to financial instability once the debt became too great. The clincher for me was when David explained that by merely investing $20,000 to start the business, for instance, I could expect to earn $6,000 in additional income each month. Who wouldn't want to earn $6,000 each month by simply investing $20,000? It was a no-brainer. I thought to myself, "I could easily break even in less than four months." This certainly piqued my curiosity and I listened more intently from that moment on. I could actually visualize the dollars signs in my head.

The fourth expectation was *decision making*. David explained that a decision maker is someone who takes action. So, I had to ask myself if I was willing (yes or no) to decide *that day* to take action and move forward with affiliate marketing. He asked me to think about how much I wanted to earn after three months, after six months, and then after one year. I quickly thought about it, and determined that earning $25,000 after three months, $50,000 after six months, and $100,000 after one year all seemed reasonable. David agreed without any hesitation. But, as I pointed out earlier, all thinking and reasoning become a blur once you've been hooked. There is no turning back. I wanted to be a decision maker on that very day. I wanted to take action. Although I had practically convinced myself that this was something I wanted in on, I still hadn't pulled out my credit card. I still wanted to hear more. David proceeded to tell me more about the business, and the more he talked the more determined I became. He was a very fast talker. Reflecting back, I imagine that David's job suddenly became easier after convincing me to become a decision maker. Sadly, it didn't even take long for him to convince me. I have no doubt that he was feeling really smug about his accomplishments of piquing my interest and hooking another unsuspecting soul. How foolish of me back then.

GETTING DOWN TO BUSINESS

David assured me that I would learn all about affiliate marketing through their online trainings, instructional videos, e-library tools, and from their coaching staff. But first, homework! I was told to watch a video which introduced and provided an overview of affiliate marketing. When I was learning about this type of marketing strategy, two different methods were discussed; one that required a website, and one that did not. The pros for establishing and maintaining a website far outnumbered the pros for not having one. Again, this piqued my interest, and I was drawn in even more. After all, by having my own website, as David clearly laid out, I would be able to build an email list, create saleable assets, access cash on demand, maintain longevity, and it would be easy to leverage. I was eager to learn more. For me personally, this meant purchasing a new computer because I couldn't possibly perform all the required tasks that could build my business by using my current antiquated computer. At that moment, I envisioned myself in my home office, diligently working on a new, fast, and efficient computer. I also thought about the cost of this new computer; maybe $1,200-$1,400? Regardless of the cost, I knew I needed to start shopping.

I continued to watch the video that was assigned to me as if I were watching my favorite TV show. There were three types of affiliate marketing discussed: pay-per-sale, pay-per-action, and pay-per-click, which was not very popular according to the video. So, why go with the least popular affiliate marketing strategy, right? Pay-per-click was the only affiliate marketing strategy that I previously knew about, but not a whole lot. The other two seemed very appealing so I zeroed in on them and took detailed notes. I instantly knew that I wanted to me a part of the action.

The second video covered the "Ingredients of Success." There were various clips of individuals who provided testimonials about their successful affiliate marketing and dropshipping businesses. They were all very convincing; just regular, ordinary people who were making thousands of dollars each week through e-marketing, and willing to share their success stories. So, I thought, "If these regular, ordinary people were able to be successful in a relatively short period of time, why can't I?"

There were three levels of investment explained by David, and the cost associated with each one. But, as David phrased it, "I wouldn't just be buying an investment, I would be buying the relationship." The three levels of investment consisted of:

1) $6,500 (no website provided)
2) $9,800 (build your own website)
3) $12,600 (custom-built website)

I knew absolutely nothing about building a website and I couldn't understand how running a marketing business without a website would be beneficial, but the cost of a custom-built website was far too pricey. Given how I felt about this, David explained that their company would custom-build my website for the amazing cost of only $9,800. This was music to my ears, so I chose this level of investment. David further explained that this cost would also include coaching sessions, and that my website would be up and running in about three weeks. Again, music to my ears.

The next order of business was to do some brainstorming activities to determine how I wanted to approach my affiliate marketing business, and the type of goals I wished to establish. I was instructed to list my hobbies, my interests, what I had done for a living over the years, the magazines that I subscribed to, the clubs and organizations that I belonged to, my pets (which I didn't have), the skills that I currently possessed, skills that I would like to possess, the vehicle(s) that I drove, and lastly my goals and dreams. Then, the all-important question that I needed to answer was, "If I could do anything for work, what would it be?" I completed this exercise but was a little unsure of how it related. My goal or dream was simply to earn a six-figure salary and live a debt-free, financially secure lifestyle. *I guess this is the American dream for a lot of people.* As for the type of work that I would choose to do above anything else, it was to buy older homes, remodel or renovate them, and then rent them out to generate additional income, creating positive cash flow. It all sounded like a good plan.

Then entered Tony, another player in Jennifer's party of deceit. I believe Tony was a sales associate with Prime Corporate Services, and he was deemed my "go-to" person. I felt pretty special at first, because Tony had given me his direct email address and telephone number. He would get back in touch with me on October 20, 2017, at 3 p.m. But for the time being, it was all about the business of establishing my Limited Liability Company (LLC). I had no idea what I was getting myself into, but it all sounded interesting, and I didn't want to miss out on this opportunity. Establishing an LLC would, according to Tony, provide protection and tax benefits (profit and loss). It would limit my liability, I would own 100 percent of my business, and I could avoid paying self-employment taxes. Most importantly, Tony explained that I would be able to build wealth and be able to write off the entire amount of my start-up costs and expenses at tax time. Shortly thereafter, I would be provided with a Tax ID number and an Employee Identification Number.

PHASE ONE

There were two phases that I had to complete. Phase one was all about devoting 20-26 hours per week to my ecommerce business (15 hours initially). According to Tony, there were two ways of building wealth with my ecommerce business: dropshipping and affiliate marketing. Extensive training, I was told, would be provided for both. Tony briefly described each one and explained that dropshipping would yield a higher income percentage than affiliate marketing alone.

Essentially, with dropshipping, I would list items or products on my website, place orders for clients who were interested in buying, and then have those items shipped out to the clients. With affiliate marketing, however, I would market other people's products and drive traffic to their website where customers would hopefully buy the products. It all seemed so simple at that time. Clearly, I could do both!

PHASE TWO

Phase two was all about choosing a niche, and I was told to complete that task by the following week. It entailed reviewing my brainstorming activities, researching my chosen niche, researching the demand, and assessing the competition. This phase turned out to be a very tedious and time-consuming process. During the interim, I was told that a Business Credit Advisor would be in touch with me to discuss the process of starting a business line of credit in order to produce a PAYDEX score. *What?* I had never heard of a PAYDEX score. "How was this different from a FICO score," I wondered. I was now thinking to myself that I needed to first, build a website, then market products to be dropshipped and/or use the affiliate marketing approach, establish an LLC, and then establish a business line of credit to produce a PAYDEX score. It was a lot to take in. I didn't realize it then, but Tony's pitch about establishing a business line of credit was actually paving the way for other products and services that he and his associates wanted me to purchase. How much was all of this going to cost? Could I afford it all?

Sure, I had some pressing concerns, but I still wanted in. I wanted to hear more and learn more, even though the cost of these programs and coaching sessions had not been revealed yet. I could have interjected and asked Tony to cut to the chase and tell me the cost, but I didn't. I still don't know why I didn't ask, but I wonder if it would have changed my decision if I had.

After Tony thoroughly explained the purpose of a PAYDEX score and how it was tied to a business line of credit, unlike a FICO score that's tied to a personal line of credit, I quickly understood why it would be important to separate business credit from personal credit. Tony further explained that the goal was to keep more money in my pocket, mainly because business interest rates were low. Having business credit would separate financial liability and allow for my business to pay for itself. Tax advisors would be available to speak with me as often as needed. Additionally, by purchasing the Business Credit Program, it would allow me to work with advisors to develop a good PAYDEX score. Tony had a great pitch.

ENROLLMENT FEES ADDING UP

My first task, of course, was to create a Limited Liability Company, and there were two options available. There was the $1,660 option and the $2,950 option which would be more beneficial, according to Tony. It all happened so fast. Before I knew it, I began receiving and signing electronic service agreements for all the services and programs that were presented by David and Tony. Additionally, I had to create an ID that was unique only to me, such as a password. Moving forward, my unique ID would be revealed to me each time someone from their team contacted me by phone. I was instructed to never talk to anyone who did not know my unique ID. I chose "20 Touchdown" as my unique ID.

I asked myself, "What was the real purpose of the unique ID? Also, Did David and Tony already know about all my credit cards and the available credit I had on each one?" Based on the questions they asked me at the onset, it seemed as if they already had prior knowledge of my zero credit card balances, the limit on each credit card, and my current FICO score which was above 800. "Did they ask me certain questions about my credit situation only to confirm what they already knew?" I had a strange feeling about it all, but I proceeded to enroll in the programs nonetheless.

The enrollment agreement for the initial investment was delivered to me electronically on October 10, 2017, by Web Market Services. The description of the products and services that I would receive was rather extensive, so it would cause anyone to believe that their money would be well-spent. A lot of "buzz words" were used in the description such as: platinum, custom, optimized, SEO friendly, kick fire gold marketing, technical support, lister labs, eBay software, professional research, in-depth research, weekly coaching sessions, unlimited access, live webinars, and industry experts. Oh, but wait – the monthly hosting/membership fee was $39.95, and this fee would be waived for the first 90 days after my enrollment. *Lucky me!*

Cost of the initial investment charged to my credit card: **$9,800**

On October 20, 2017, I received another enrollment agreement, and it was from Prime Corporate Services, LLC for the initiation of service: LLC Entity Set-Up. It described how Prime Corporate Services would establish a Limited Liability Company on my behalf. They would draw up and file the Articles of Organization and file the necessary documents to obtain my Employer Identification Number (EIN) for tax purposes. Since I knew nothing about setting up an LLC, I felt that this would be a wise investment. I chose my entity name – BTK Unlimited Concepts, **LLC**. Everything else was taken care of, which included registering my LLC with the State of Nevada and obtaining my State Business License.

Cost of this LLC Entity Set-Up charged to my credit card: **$1,600**

The next enrollment agreement I received from Prime Corporate Services on October 20, 2017, was for the Executive Corporate Credit Package. The title alone sounded prominent. I felt important and worthy. This agreement included twelve weeks of scheduled coaching sessions, phone and email support for 12 months, guidance on *How to Become Business Competent*, access to an extensive business compliance report, access to an extensive list of credit reporting vendors, and a welcome call and welcome email within 24 hours of signing up.

Cost of this Corporate Credit Package charged to my credit card: **$2,950**

Shortly thereafter, on October 26, 2017, I received a phone call at home from a representative, encouraging me to purchase another program that was being offered by Prime Corporate Services. I was caught completely off guard, but by that time, I was thinking that in order to achieve success and get to that next level, I needed to take full advantage of everything that their company was offering. And, just like that, I was signing another purchase agreement to enroll in their Tax Preparation Program. Again, the description of the program would cause anyone to believe that it would be a wise investment. It was also filled with buzz words such as: consultations, permanent account manager, unlimited tax support, federal tax form preparations, quarterly tax filings, representation if audited, and reimbursements in cases of mistakes on tax forms. Oh, and that's not all – this tax preparation program came with a monthly fee of $34.95 and this fee was due to begin January 1, 2018. If I had only read the fine print more carefully, I would have known about the $329.99 annual renewal fee that was due to begin January 15, 2019, unless I canceled in writing prior to that date.

Cost of this Tax Preparation Program charged to my credit card: **$3,890**

Things started to get really serious. All while I was purchasing the above three programs and services, I had already begun my weekly coaching sessions which I purchased through Web Market Services on October 10, 2017, for $9,800.00 (my initial investment*)*. Brad was assigned as my support coach (another player in Jennifer Shah's game). Prior to my coaching sessions, I received my welcome letter and instructions on how to access the online digital learning platform (e-library). The first phase of this program consisted of 10 weekly, 30-minute coaching sessions with Brad, with unlimited access to phone, live chat, and email support. My coaching sessions commenced on October 16, 2017. The very first session was just an overview of the two types of affiliate marketing. My homework assignment was to complete phase two of affiliate marketing, and this assignment was due before the next coaching session.

To recall, phase two of Affiliate Marketing involved brainstorming, researching a niche, researching the demand, and assessing the competition. This was a bit overwhelming, but I was determined to complete these tasks accordingly because, after all, I had to prove that I was *teachable*. I had to prove that I was willing to learn and then be able to apply what I had learned. I selected organization as my niche, mainly because I considered myself to be a highly organized person, at home and at work. I was determined to show how decluttering and organizing every room in one's home or in an office could ultimately lead to a better home and work environment. My two main categories were *home organization* and *storage solutions*.

The rest of my sessions with Coach Brad during this first phase were brutal, in that there was so much to accomplish, including a massive amount of homework assignments. These assignments consisted of the following:

- Creating an AdWords account to access and use a Google Keyword Planner
- Advertising on Google
- Understanding technical terms associated with affiliate marketing
- Determining high and low competition in relation to choosing a niche
- Using Google search tools (e.g., META title)
- Choosing a domain name for my website ($12.00 yearly domain fee)
- Setting up a Facebook business account as well as developing many other social media accounts
- Establishing a dropshipping account with Doba (Doba.com) which was not free.

So, yes – then there was Doba. The costs were quickly adding up. The second phase of this program would include email support and live chat, but no direct coaching sessions with Brad. *Imagine that!* On November 2, 2017, Brad informed me that I needed a good supplier if I intended to do dropshipping effectively, so shortly thereafter I remember speaking with Mack, a sales associate, who explained why DOBA would be a great supplier for my website. He further outlined and explained the advantages of buying a membership with Doba.com. Mack described how I could upload hundreds of products onto my website at once. He asserted that, "The buyer would always pay me first." I would then submit the buyer's order to Doba, and Doba would ship the products to the buyer. I would then keep the difference. It was basically "taking products and reselling them to others at a higher cost," according to Mack. He explained that the products had to be of "good quality" and the "profit margins also had to be good" in order to make money. He stressed that the neat thing about Doba was that their inventory of products was already sourced and available in their data base catalog where I would have 24/7 access. Mack said, "Since there were 1.8 million items on Doba.com, I was sure to find the products that I needed for my website. Better yet, I would receive training on how to upload products from Doba.com, onto my website." But as usual, everything comes at a hefty cost, as outlined below:

1-Year Membership: ~~$4,000~~ – Special Price, **$2,500**
2-Year Membership: ~~$6,000~~ – Special Price, **$4,000**
4-Year Membership: ~~$8,000~~ – Special Price, **$5,500**

I ended up purchasing the one-year membership. After already spending a boatload of money on all the other programs and services that I had purchased up to that point, it just made better sense to choose the least expensive membership plan. I received my welcome call from a sales associate with Doba.com on November 14, 2017, who walked me through the basics. I immediately got to work, using the export tools to load products from Doba.com onto my website. I started by determining my categories which were: home, garden, and living, home improvement storage and organization, and kitchen storage and organization. From there, I developed the subcategories on my website, such as bedroom storage, storage baskets, craft storage, travel storage, office storage, and shoe cabinet storage. I then began the painstaking uploading process. It was not nearly as simple as Mack had described. It instead was a very lengthy, tedious, and tiresome process. My work hours started to quickly add up. By that time, I was easily dedicating 60-70 grueling hours each week to my business, which was well past the 10-15 hours per week that David had originally specified. It was all very taxing, given the overlapping homework assignments I had to complete for all my coaches. I was completely swamped.

Cost of this dropshipping membership charged to my credit card: **$2,500**

I completed and filed my retirement paperwork around this time as well. My retirement from the school district would become official by the end of December. On December 4, 2017, my website, BridgeOverClutter.com was fine-tuned and up and running. It was custom-built by Embark as promised. I can't describe how excited I was to have my very own website and to soon begin my ecommerce business. Brad reminded me about the $39.99 monthly hosting fee (also charged to my credit card), and that their Builder Support Team would assist me with any website software issues or questions. I continued to load products that corresponded with my selected niche onto my website from Doba.com (organization/storage solution products). The other tasks that I needed to set up on my website for dropshipping purposes included the shipping settings, payment settings, tax settings, and email forwarding settings. I would then be able to complete a test order and market my website.

Sadly, the test order that I completed on my website the following month did not yield good results. This process entailed selecting an inexpensive product on my site (product loaded from Doba.com), processing the payment, and having it shipped to my home address. I opted to buy a very cute and stylish shoe storage bag for travel. It cost roughly $26.00. The bags came in various colors, so I selected the color I wanted, and then proceeded to check-out by paying for the item with my credit card, along with the shipping cost, and arranged to have the item shipped to my home address. I received my order confirmation number right away. It was a smooth process, until it wasn't. I waited and waited for my shoe bag to arrive in the mail. It took several weeks, and that beautiful, stylish shoe bag that I uploaded from Doba.com, looked nothing like the one that arrived in the mail. It was a total disappointment! Not only did this shoe bag *not* have an outside compartment as depicted on Doba.com, but the overall style of the bag was completely different. The material was cheap and flimsy, and it lacked appeal. It seemed to be worth only about half the amount I paid. *If this had happened to a real customer, I thought, it would not have ended well for me. People want what they pay for and not a cheap imitation.*

The other annoying problem that I had with Doba.com was the unavailability of products in their inventory. I opted to receive (on a regular basis) an inventory of notification updates from Doba.com, detailing the products that were discontinued or out-of-stock. These were products that I had previously uploaded from Doba.com onto my website. Each time I received the inventory list with the updates, I had to go into my website and remove the products that were discontinued, out-of-stock, or low in inventory. It wasn't necessarily the fault of Doba.com. Nonetheless, it was nearly impossible to keep up with all the changes. *So overwhelming and so frustrating!*

I turned my attention toward building and enhancing my website and being able to drive traffic to my site. Brad reminded me that since my website had been completed by their website builders, I would be moving into the next phase of the program which was marketing. I was eager to get started. Unfortunately, this marketing phase that I was about to embark upon also came at a very hefty cost.

On December 18, 2017, I received a phone call from an associate with Mastery Pro Group, outlining their marketing program and its cost. "More and more money," I thought to myself.

I nervously asked myself, "When will it all end?" But what was I going to do, especially now? I knew nothing about marketing and driving visitors to my website to buy my products. Alas, I had no other choice but to take the call and listen. Admittedly, this particular marketing program immediately grabbed my attention because it included the following:

1) Social Media Marketing – **plus**,
2) YouTube Video Marketing – **premium**, and
3) Four marketing coaching sessions, plus four free sessions.

Notice the descriptive words, **plus** and **premium**. These two words alone led me to believe that this training would surely surpass any ordinary training. I was headed for the big times! I was somewhat hesitant at first about purchasing the program once I learned the cost, but these two words laid all my doubts to rest. I knew I needed to complete this next phase of the marketing program in order to move forward. If I didn't purchase the program, where would that leave me? Would I be able to effectively self-educate myself about social media marketing and YouTube marketing? Where would I even begin? My doubts quickly vanished, and I took the leap and agreed to purchase this marketing program.

Cost of this marketing program and coaching sessions charged to my credit card: **$8,495**

CHAPTER TWO
THE PRESSURE

It was hard for me to wrap my head around the fact that I had just accumulated $29,235 in credit card debt in a matter of two months. The last transaction was completed on December 18, 2017, and Christmas was just around the corner. I was in knee-deep now. It was like being in quicksand and I was slowing sinking to the bottom, little-by-little. There was no way of pulling myself out. I kept telling myself that I was in it for the long haul. There was no escaping now. Yes, my credit card debt was out-of-control, but I had to keep pushing ahead. I couldn't give up now.

The final homework assignments given to me by Coach Brad entailed setting up and using Google Analytics to learn how to monitor my website's statistics. This allowed me to determine where my traffic was coming from, what visitors were doing at my site, how long they were remaining on my site, and so much more. It was all so overwhelming and enthralling at the same time. Although I continued to complete my assignments on time, all I could think about was my credit card debt, and my plummeting FICO score. The minimum payments on the three cards that I had used to purchase all of the programs and services were totaling into the hundreds.

My coaching sessions with Brad were nearing an end. I was instructed to contact other available coaches for website support, via chat or email, once my time officially ended with Brad. It was recommended beforehand that I watch some marketing videos in their e-library at webmarketservices.biz, prior to the start of my marketing sessions with my new coach. On December 18, 2017, I received an email from Mastery Pro Group, asking that I call their office to set up appointments for my upcoming coaching sessions. I did so right away, and I was assigned Coach Kevin, *another one of Jennifer Shah's associates*. The first of the four marketing sessions that I would engage in with Coach Kevin was due to begin Wednesday, December 20, 2017. As with Coach Brad, these coaching sessions would run about 25-30 minutes, via telephone. My last few sessions with Coach Brad overlapped with my sessions with Coach Kevin. It was a lot to take in and a lot of moving parts.

Then it struck me like a brick; just four sessions for $8,495? I was expecting more, but at the same time, I was thinking that these were described as plus and premium marketing sessions. So, I was getting "the cream-of-the-crop"! Plus, I would receive four FREE coaching sessions. According to Jacob, one of the support coaches with Mastery Pro Group, I would only have to make minimum payments on my credit cards for about 3-4 months. Afterwards, I would be able to make larger payments after my business grew. This was the 'Gospel' according to Jacob. Jacob added that it would take 90 – 120 days to get my business up and running. It all made sense at that time. I wanted so badly to believe him.

It didn't take long, however, for reality to set in. Looking back, everything that I learned in those four coaching sessions with Coach Kevin, was already available on YouTube tutorials for *free*. This was not the plus and premium level material that I had expected from Coach Kevin. There is no secret that YouTube has countless number of video tutorials on the differences between Search Engine

Optimization (SEO) and Search Media Optimization (SMO), tutorials on using social bookmarking websites, creating accounts with Google Plus and Twitter, and tutorials on using social media to drive traffic to one's website. I was just oblivious to the social media networking and marketing material that was available back then. Kevin seized this opportunity. I was already his "mark", and he took full advantage. *A grifter has a powerful grip.*

The four, weekly coaching sessions with Kevin began December 20, 2017, and ended January 10, 2018. Really? Four sessions for $8,495? In actuality, I never did receive those four free coaching sessions that had been promised. This was unnerving! The sessions and homework assignments focused mainly on creating accounts on social bookmarking websites (e.g., Stumbleupon.com, Reddit.com, Digg.com*),* and using certain techniques to get my stories, articles, or blogs optimized for those social bookmarking sites. It was a lot to digest, with a lot of time spent on social media platforms, reading, commenting, posting on Facebook, sharing posts, blogging, liking, following, tweeting, re-tweeting, linking keywords, linking phrases, bookmarking, adding favorites, and then repeating it all several times each week.

Again, most of what I learned from Coach Kevin was available for free on YouTube. I suspected that the cost of the four coaching sessions would be exorbitant, but after learning the actual cost, I chose to buy the program regardless. Why didn't I do my due diligence? After all, I did have 72 hours to cancel my contract with Mastery Pro Group. Why didn't I act on this?

Oh, but wait – there was still more to come. I was told by another associate to expect a follow-up phone call from Jacob or another team member during the early part of January. So, on January 11, 2018, I received a phone call from Caleb, an associate with Mastery Pro Group. He boasted a little about having been in the ecommerce business for 10 years; starting first with eBay and then with Amazon. He talked about how starting a business line of credit could be beneficial for safeguarding my business. He went on to describe the additional *fourteen live marketing coaching sessions* that I could buy with Coach Kevin through Mastery Pro Group, for the low, low cost of $5,995 (normally $7,999). Caleb assured me that this would be my final cost. These sessions would be a continuation of marketing and selling products, focusing mainly on linking products to my website and selling on eBay.

Theoretically, I would be getting more coaching sessions for a lower price than the previous four sessions, so I went for it. What was wrong with me? Again, YouTube has plenty of tutorials on how to upload a video, how to market products on your website via Pinterest and other platforms by linking images, tutorials on how to use eBay and PayPal calculations to analyze and determine prices for products to sell on eBay, how to complete a profit market analysis of your products, and tutorials on how to list, estimate shipping costs, and sell your products on eBay. Once again, I didn't do my due diligence.

I became distraught and nervous while speaking with Caleb about this final step and final cost of the program. I began to really question the legitimacy of the program. Yet, Caleb was very cunning and convinced me to move forward with the purchase. And, just like that, I agreed, but this decision led to nothing but more worry and regret. The next few days were terrifying. I began to sweat uncontrollably, my heart pounded, I grew weaker, was in tears, grew weary during the day, and was unable to sleep at night. I was disappointed in myself for agreeing to purchase the fourteen coaching sessions, but I felt like I didn't have a choice if I wanted to build my business and start earning money. My judgement was undoubtedly clouded.

Cost of this second marketing program and coaching sessions charged to my credit card: **$5,955**

Things started to get somewhat complicated from that point on. My coaching sessions with Kevin were overlapping with sessions I was receiving with another coach. In order to illustrate how certain events unfolded and how intricate they quickly became, I would have to first go back (or take you back) several weeks. During the early part in December of 2017, I received a phone call from Colby, *another one of Jennifer Shah's associates*. Colby was a Corporate Credit Coach with Prime Corporate Services, and he began working with me to establish a business line of credit. Oh, yes – another program, but I had already purchased this "Executive Corporate Credit Package" back on October 20, 2017, for $2,950. It was now time to put things in motion. According to Coach Colby, I needed to establish a major business line of credit. In order to establish this credit, I needed to use my Business Entity Name, *BTK Unlimited Concepts, LLC,* to first open four smaller credit accounts with select vendors.

Colby then talked about how it was essential that I establish a D-U-N-S number by first setting up my company's profile (BTK Unlimited Concepts, LLC) with Dun and Bradstreet. All of this was foreign to me, so I just went with the flow. The entire process required multiple steps to obtain a D-U-N-S number and to open four smaller accounts to help build my business credit score (Paydex Score), and credit worthiness. Colby sent me an article to read entitled, "Using Vendor Transactions to Build Business Credit". My brain was overloaded by this time, and I started to feel the pressure building.

The next step was to apply for a business account with at least three vendors. Colby sent me a list of vendors, via email, and instructed me to apply with at least three of them. I proceeded to contact these vendors and received feedback rather quickly. Without hesitation, I officially applied and opened accounts in December of 2017 with the following four vendors: Chevron/Texaco, Office Depot/Office Max, Staples, and Quill.com. Colby instructed me to make at least one modest purchase each month from each vendor, and to make my payments on time or early. This was crucial because timely payments would "yield an excellent Paydex Score," according to Colby.

Over the next few months, I went on to make modest purchases on each account each month. I paid off the balance on each account prior to the due dates, just as instructed. Most of my purchases included office supplies (e.g., paper, notepads, desk organizers, folders, binders). In most cases, I didn't even need these products, but I purchased them regardless to help build my business credit score (Paydex score). Even though I paid off the balance with each vendor at the end of each month, these costs quickly added up.

Nevertheless, all of my efforts seemed to pay off at first because I successfully received my Dun & Bradstreet D-U-N-S number for my entity, BTK Unlimited Concepts, LLC. This would later make it possible for me to apply for a business line of credit with a major credit card company (I later chose Chase Bank Business Ink). The goal, according to Colby, was to transfer the balances from my other credit cards over to my Business Credit Card(s). Unfortunately, there was one hiccup, and this occurred soon after a very devastating event.

STRESS OVERLOAD

The stress was entirely too much for me to bear. On January 14, 2018, I suffered a mild heart attack and had to be hospitalized. It was a very scary period. Prior to my heart attack, I was in good, physical health. I was not taking any prescription medications. A few days leading up to my heart attack, I was working on building my business credit score with the guidance of Coach Colby, and I had just finished my fourth coaching session with Kevin on January 10, 2018. During that particular session, Kevin focused entirely on Twitter. For homework, Kevin instructed me to *tweet* once a day, share three other people's tweets, and comment on their tweets. I did not have a Twitter account at that time, and I knew nothing about *tweeting*, so Kevin suggested that I should go to the e-library on their company's website to access and watch tutorial videos on Twitter and Google Plus. These tutorials were very general, so I expressed my concerns to Kevin about this the following day. I needed step-by-step instructions (specifics) on how to *tweet* and use Google Plus effectively, and the video tutorials were not providing me with what I needed. It was such a frustrating time. I think it was designed that way so that Mastery Pro Group could justify the need for the additional fourteen coaching sessions. I believe it was part of the con game.

During the morning of my heart attack on January 14th, I was watching YouTube videos to try and teach myself more about Twitter and **Google Plus**. I knew I needed to do this to complete my homework assignment of tweeting daily, sharing three others' tweets, and commenting on their tweets. I was also concentrating on writing my next blog to post on my website. At the same time, I was thinking about how foolish I had been for purchasing the fourteen coaching sessions. I was becoming overwhelmingly stressed. I remember the pressure building in my left arm; the sweating, the lightheadedness, the inability to focus, the unusual, awkward feeling in my entire body, and the pounding of my heart. It was a frightening feeling, but I really didn't know what was happening at first. I immediately stopped what I was doing and called the 24-Hour nurse hotline. I was instructed to go to urgent care right away.

Shortly after arriving at urgent care and having my vitals taken, the staff performed an EKG which showed some irregularities. My blood test revealed elevated troponin levels and my blood pressure was also elevated. As described by *Medlineplus.com*,

> Troponin is a type of protein found in the muscles of your heart. Troponin isn't normally found in the blood. When heart muscles become damaged, troponin is sent into the bloodstream. As heart damage increases, greater amounts of troponin are released in the blood.

Due to the seriousness of my condition, an ambulance was ordered, and I was immediately whisked off to the emergency room at the nearest hospital, where I was admitted right away. It was all so surreal. The following day, I had to undergo an exploratory procedure to determine if there was any damage to my heart. Thankfully, there was no damage. I was diagnosed with Takotsubo Syndrome, and it's brought on by stress, according to the doctors. It's also known as the "Broken Heart Syndrome." More specifically, "It occurs when a person experiences sudden acute stress that can rapidly weaken the heart muscles," as defined by Ilan Shor Wittstein, M.D.

The doctors and nurses who treated me were deeply concerned and wanted to know what had caused me so much stress. I told them about the online home-based business that I had recently purchased and how I believed I was a victim of a scam. They seemed genuinely concerned. They told me that I needed to find a way to control my stress to avoid another episode. I vowed to try, but I really didn't know how or where to begin. I just prayed that I would find some solutions. They warned me that high levels of troponin in my blood could cause damage to my heart. The staff checked my troponin levels regularly during my stay at the hospital. The attending doctor could not release me from the hospital until my troponin levels were within normal range. Finally, my levels started to normalize, and I was released shortly after 2 p.m. on January 15, 2018. The doctor prescribed the four following medications that I needed to take daily after my discharge:

1) Aspirin – blood thinner
2) Atorvastatin (Lipitor) – to lower cholesterol
3) Carvedilol – beta blocker
4) Lisinopril (Zestril) – to control high blood pressure

I was assured by the doctor that these medications were typically prescribed to individuals following a cardiac event. Collectively, they could reduce the risk of death after a future heart attack. Going forward, I had to think about ways to protect my heart and to avoid having another episode. Shortly after my release from the hospital, I adopted a new way of thinking and I started practicing various calming techniques to help control my stress. Additionally, I followed up with a cardiologist that was appointed to me upon my discharge. This would become an ongoing cardiologist visit, every six months. So, just like that, my overall health was forever changed. Still, I refused to give up. I made a commitment to my business, and I was determined to follow through. Besides, there was too much at stake. My total investment, thus far, had approached $35,290; all charged to my credit cards.

BACK TO THE GRIND

My coaching sessions with Kevin resumed on January 17, 2018. Since I was determined to show my coach that I was indeed teachable, I needed to refocus and concentrate on building my business as quickly as possible. I worried that my FICO score would continue to fall, so I needed to make money fast to pay off my debt. Time was of the essence! I went straight to work following my hospitalization, without fully recuperating, and completed the arduous tasks of listing and selling products on eBay. I listed a few items from my website and even listed items that I had lying around my house, as Coach Kevin had suggested (approximately eight items altogether). After spending countless hours and days analyzing products and performing eBay and PayPal calculations for all my products, none of the products from my website sold, and I only sold three of the products that were lying around my house. The first item, which was a ceiling fan and light medallion, sold for $18.81 but cost me $15.14 to ship. I originally purchased this item at a local home improvement store, and it was still in its original, unopened package. The second item I sold was a bead jewelry designer starter kit. It sold for $21.00 but cost me $15.33 to ship. I originally purchased this jewelry kit at a local craft store, and it was still in its original, unopened package. The third item that I sold on eBay was a set of car seat covers – *premium*. They sold for $25.00 but cost me $15.33 to ship. I originally purchased the seat covers at a local auto center and, like the other items, the seat covers were still in their original, unopened package. Technically, I didn't earn any profits from these sales because the shipping costs swallowed up all the profits, and I originally paid more for the items than what they sold for. I was not off to a good start! All of my efforts amounted to nothing. But I kept thinking and repeating a famous quote to myself, "Stay calm and press on."

After all of the work that I put into social media marketing, creating and posting a video on YouTube, creating links, analyzing, listing and selling products on eBay, using doba.com to sell products, using Pinterest and other platforms, etc., I still had not earned any money after four months of trying. I was deeply worried. *Could there be another way to create profits? Is there something I'm missing?*

I didn't want to toss in the towel just yet, but it grew more and more difficult for me to accomplish the tasks or assignments that were given to me by my coaches. Suddenly, without any warning, I was unable to log into the business side (the backend) of my website. I tried for three days without any success, so I sent an email to the Builder Technical Support Team about this issue on February 25, 2018. They responded immediately, apologized, and stated that they were having some technical difficulties with godaddy.com, their domain platform. They requested my username and password for the purpose of resetting or updating my "name servers." I barely understood their explanation, but I gave them my credentials anyhow. The support team assured me that they were working with godaddy.com and their developers to get this issue revolved as quickly as possible. During the interim, I focused my attention on other pressing matters.

TAX SEASON BLUES

Tax time was approaching, so I wanted to file my 2017 taxes as soon as possible. I was confident that I would receive a substantial tax refund. Since I had already purchased the Tax Preparation Program on October 20, 2017, for $3,890, I wanted to take full advantage of this service right away through Tax Sentry, Inc. Their monthly fee of $34.95 had already commenced (January of 2018) and payments had already been charged to my credit card. I reminded myself that I would be able to write off the entire start-up costs for my business on my tax return, as promised by the representative who sold me this tax preparation program. "Finally," I thought. "Something to look forward to!" I was elated about the possibility of receiving a substantial tax refund. So, on March 8, 2018, I signed two letters of engagement (terms of agreement) with Tax Sentry, Inc. – BTA Accounting and Tax Prep. One of the engagement letters granted BTA Accounting permission to prepare my individual tax return and the other my business tax return. I was eager to get started! I signed, dated, and returned both engagements letters to Beverly at Tax Sentry right away. Yes, Beverly – another player in the con game.

Shortly thereafter, Beverly sent me tax organizers and worksheets, via email, for the purpose of gathering the necessary information for my tax return. The organizers and worksheets were extensive, but I expected that. When I began to complete the Business Income and Expenses worksheet, I marveled at how thorough this worksheet was and how easy it was to complete because of the prelisted items. So, I began to record the dollar amounts that I spent in 2017 for each of the prelisted items, as detailed below.

Computer purchase:	*$1,040*
Consulting / training:	*$14,490*
Website design fees:	*$74*
Entity creation (cost for LLC set up):	*$1,660*
Business permits / fees:	*$15*
Interest paid to banks, etc.:	*$212*
Website creation / internet:	*$9,800*
Legal and professional (ex. Tax Sentry):	*$3,949*
Licenses (annual dues for LLC):	*$200*
Office expenses / supplies:	*$100*
Other interest (credit card interest):	*$250*
Telephone (cell phone or business):	*$130*
Wholesale / drop shipper fees:	*$2,500*
Other:	*$2,950*

I also provided information about my "Business Use of Home" on the worksheet (e.g., size of my home, square footage of home office, utilities spent, etc.). I thought of every possible deduction and included them on the worksheet. I felt satisfied with my accomplishments. As for my individual income tax form, I listed my usual deductions on the worksheet, which was also extensive because I owned two homes (primary residence and rental property). I also worked part-time as a licensed real estate agent, so there was a good amount for me to itemize from both businesses.

After I completed and submitted my organizers and worksheets to Tax Sentry, via secured email, I waited, and waited, and waited for the completion of my taxes. Then, a representative from Tax Sentry explained that there would be a delay in filing my tax returns. The delay had nothing to do with anything that I had done, so I couldn't understand the reason behind the delay. BTA Accounting would go on to file my federal income taxes after the April 1st tax deadline date, and to make matters worse, I did not receive a refund. Instead, I ended up owing the IRS $84. This was another costly blow.

Nothing made sense anymore. What was the purpose of purchasing a Tax Preparation Program for $3,800, with a monthly fee of $34.95 and an annual fee of $329.99? How was I benefiting from this program? Couldn't a regular tax preparation service do the same thing as Tax Sentry for far less money – perhaps thousands less? After all, the most I had ever paid to a company to prepare my taxes was roughly $400. This was a far-cry from $3,800! *What was wrong with me?* I began questioning every single component of my ecommerce business. The sessions with Colby, my corporate credit coach, were overlapping with my sessions with Kevin. I didn't get a tax refund after everything I had invested into the business. It was suddenly becoming a tangled mess.

BUSINESS CREDIT WOES

Coach Colby sent me an email on April 2, 2018, congratulating me for completing Phase 1 of the Business Credit Program. He attached a list of 0% Annual Percentage Rate business credit cards that I could apply for. Was I ready to take this next step? If I open up another line of credit, wouldn't this hurt my credit score? The sole purpose for having business credit cards was to eliminate the debt on my personal credit cards by transferring the balances from those cards over to my business credit cards. Seemed simple, right? Why was I hesitant? Was it really that simple?

Moving into Phase 2 of the Business Credit Program meant that my scheduled telephone sessions with Colby was coming to an end. Colby assured me, however, that I would have continued access to the coaches by way of emails and telephone contacts to address any questions or concerns as I continued to build my business credit profile. He went on to state that Dun & Bradstreet offered two free services through their interface, and that I could possibly activate them both. Fortunately, I had already signed up for these services, so moving forward, I would be able to get regular updates about my business credit and keep track of my Paydex score. I was one step closer to eliminating my personal credit card debt. *Or at least I thought I was.*

As stated earlier in this chapter, opening smaller accounts with those four vendors would later make it possible for me to apply for a business line of credit with a major credit card company. The goal, according to Colby, was to transfer the balances from my personal credit cards to my business credit card account. I applied for several business credit cards but was only approved by Chase Bank Business Ink. To make matters worse, Chase Business Ink would only allow me to do a balance transfer of $5,000. I still, therefore, had approximately $30,000.00 in personal credit card debt to pay down.

A CHANGE OF SCENERY

I was getting closer and closer to calling it quits. I vacillated between tossing in the towel or staying firm and riding it out. It was also during this time that I was toiling with the idea of selling my primary residence and relocating. One of the benefits of owning your own home-based business is that you can operate your business from any location where there's good Wi-Fi. I thought about how cool it would be to live on one of the Hawaiian Islands and operate my business from that location. *How fun it would be to wake up each morning in paradise and choose if I wanted to work or not work that day. Could I actually build my business to a level where I could choose to work that day or take the day off and enjoy the splendor of Hawaii?* I was on it. I was game!

I booked a fight to the Big Island of Hawaii in April of 2018, and planned a one-week stay. Soon afterwards, I found myself touring available homes with a local real estate agent who showed me properties that were moderately priced, mostly newly constructed homes in Hilo. The downside to living in certain communities in Hilo is its close proximity to the active Kilauea and Mauna Loa volcanos. There are nine Lava-Flow Hazard Zones in Hawaii. Zone 1 represents the areas that are most hazardous and Zone 9 the least hazardous, as defined by Wikipedia.org. Most of the homes that I toured were situated in Lava Zone 3, hence their affordability. Still, I seriously entertained the idea of living in Hawaii and running my ecommerce business from there. Better yet, my younger sister intended to relocate to Hawaii with me. She lived in Massachusetts at that time. Truthfully, it was her idea and dream from the very beginning. I was determined to make it a reality. I would first buy the house, and we would then live together and split the costs after she secured employment. We had it all mapped out.

MORE LETDOWNS

Unfortunately, the dreamed died about two weeks after I returned from Hawaii when Kilauea volcano erupted. It destroyed over 700 homes, most of which were in the same communities where I had toured properties. This was a very sad occasion, especially for those effected firsthand by the volcano's destruction. I now needed a Plan B. When one door closes, another one opens. But will that open door lead to the fulfillment of my dreams and goals, or to a long, dark path of destruction?

I had some major concerns and questions I needed answers to once I resumed my business activities. On April 18, 2018, I shared my concerns with Kevin during our coaching session. I expressed how I was counting on dropshipping with doba.com to be my main money-maker. I then explained why I was so deeply frustrated with the dropshipping program. I told Kevin that it would be nearly impossible to sell Doba products on my website because their retail prices or wholesale prices were too high. The profit margins, therefore, were not good. After doing further research, I discovered that Doba products were actually priced higher than most competitors. In addition, the suppliers used by Doba all had restocking fees for the products that I was trying to sell. During the entire process, I only had one inquiry from a customer about one of the products listed on my website, and that customer chose not to buy because of the restocking fee. She found the exact same product on another website that didn't have a restocking fee. This made me furious, not with the customer, but with Kevin.

I complained to Kevin that if I could not sell Doba products on my website, then the $2,500 that I paid for Doba.com would just be "money down the drain." Kevin suggested three other wholesale suppliers to explore, and I even signed up with those suppliers while on the phone with Kevin. He also suggested that I find other drop-shippers on Google.com. Lastly, he instructed me to list 10 products from these new suppliers on eBay to sell, and to email the description numbers to him. My efforts, however, did not amount to anything. It was all just a waste of valuable time, because I was unable to find the appropriate products to list on eBay for free from the new suppliers. Kevin originally stated that the suppliers were free to use, with no membership fee, but that was not the case with all the suppliers that he recommended. It was just another tactic employed by Kevin to keep me from suspecting the truth. *There was no real money to be made.* This whole process led straight to a dead end; $2,500 down the drain!

Still, I continued to try and sell my products on eBay and on my website over the next few months, praying that I would get lucky. Still, I sold no additional products, and I made absolutely *no* money. Again, I wrote and posted blogs on my website, but I got no traffic. When I thought it couldn't get any worse, I was faced with the unimaginable in April of 2018. I was completely locked out of my own website. I had no way of accessing the backend of my website to post blogs, to delete or download products from Doba.com, etc. I couldn't even locate the icon for Chat Support with Web Market

Services. I repeatedly called the Support Team, but no one returned my phone calls. I sent an email, but I did not get a response. The staff just went dark. I felt completely abandoned. It wasn't until much later that I learned that the host for my website had transitioned from Embark to Elite. This didn't make any sense to me because the paid invoice that I received from Web Market Services clearly described that their company would personally build a platinum, custom website, and use Embark Web Builder with shopping cart, SEO friendly, etc. There was a lot of technical jargon used in this description, but I got the gist of it. It was hard to believe that none of the coaches bothered to inform me about the transition beforehand.

Once the transition was finally completed, the landscape of my website was completely altered. It was unrecognizable in the worst possible way. The blogs that I had previously posted before the transition were no longer there. They were all completely swiped clean from my website. The Doba products were all jumbled up and many were missing altogether, as well as descriptions, prices, etc. This was a nightmare! The long, grueling hours that I spent writing articles, taking pictures, and posting them to my website was all for nothing. I was almost at my breaking point. I was sad and disgusted, but I had to keep it together to avoid risking another heart attack. It was evident that I was being scammed and I needed to take immediate action. I began investigating ways on how to file a formal consumer complaint. I even thought about contacting a lawyer of a pre-paid legal group that I had previously subscribed to. This would be my last resort because I first wanted to make an appeal for a refund from Web Market Services, Prime Corporate Services, and Mastery Pro Group.

I had no more drive left in me. I wanted to throw in the towel at that point because I knew that by continuing, it would cost me even more money, perhaps thousands. There would be no possible way to recuperate all my losses. There was no denying the red flags that were right in front of me. Web Market Services, Prime Corporate Services, and Mastery Pro Group were operating a fraudulent business, and they were preying on vulnerable, unsuspecting people such as myself. I needed to stop the madness. I needed to get back what they swindled from me. I needed to act fast.

CHAPTER THREE
THE DEMANDS

By May of 2018, I knew I had some hard decisions to make. *Do I continue to 'throw good money after bad,' or do I request a refund?* With my mounting credit card debt and no end in sight, I chose to request a refund. I suspected beforehand that it wouldn't be a simple task, not by a longshot. I knew that I would be met with strong resistance from all sides, but my mind was made up and there was no turning back. My primary goal was to recover as much as possible to pay down my credit card debt.

I started by requesting and signing a Temporary Hold Agreement on May 2, 2018, with Mastery Pro Group. I knew that continuing my sessions would just give me false hope. *Why torture myself? Why risk another heart attack?* It was a simple agreement stating, "By placing my training on hold with Mastery Pro Group Marketing, I agree to pause my remaining training weeks. MPG would no longer contact me on a weekly basis, and that I must contact them by phone or email to reschedule my remaining sessions." It was a statement that implied that because it was my own decision to put my training sessions on hold, I would not hold MPG Marketing accountable.

After signing the Temporary Hold Agreement, I used some time to reflect and reevaluate my situation. I needed a break. My plans to relocate to Hawaii fell through, but that didn't stop me from searching for other desirable places to spend my retirement years. *I could start over fresh, a new slate!* My search led me to Belize, so for the next few weeks, I planned to visit Belize, Central America. I signed up for a four-day tour that was offered by one of the land developers. Shortly thereafter, I flew to Belize during the first week of June to seek out new adventures. I fell in love, so I decided to buy a parcel of land to build a house on later down the road. I saw the vision! Maybe Belize was where I needed to be. Unfortunately, that decision "opened up a whole new can of worms." Another story; another time.

THE NEXT CON

After returning from Belize, I had to answer a few questions that kept haunting me. Was my ecommerce business going to propel me to great heights or would it be my downfall? Will all of my hard work pay off? I definitely had some tough decisions to make. I decided to stick to my plans and focus on recovering the money that I invested into the business. I knew that I was making the right decision because on June 22, 2018, a phone call from Jacob solidified my decision.

I knew that Jacob was eager to sell me another product because he tried calling me several times on June 18th and June 22, 2018. He sounded frantic in the voice messages that he left for me. He stated that it was important that I returned his phone call. So, I called Jacob shortly after 9:40 a.m. on June 22nd. It was concerning my website. Keep in mind that my website had been completely transformed following the transition from Embark web hosting to Elite web hosting. Just as a reminder, all of my blog posts were completely wiped out, my Doba products were jumbled and product descriptions, prices, etc. were randomly spewed all over the web pages. It was a disorderly mess. My website was once a beautifully appointed, well-organized, and very attractive website with thought-provoking articles about decluttering and organizing personal spaces. Given the name of my website, *BridgeOverClutter.com,* anyone visiting my site would expect it to be all those things I just mentioned. But, according to Jacob, my website appeared disorganized because of "errors." He specifically stated that my website had not been submitted to Elite and could not be submitted until there was a "clean-up of the codes." He directed me to look at the error codes on my website. After pulling up the codes, per Jacob' instructions, he went on to state that all the codes had to be fixed. Otherwise, my website would always appear disorganized. I jokingly referred to this part of the scam as, *"The Gospel according to Jacob!"*

I was actually afraid of what Jacob was going to say next. Was this conversation leading up to another product or service that he wanted me to purchase? If so, how much was this new product or service going to cost? What was Jacob' endgame? Jacob, once again, reiterated *my* responsibilities and the Support Team's responsibilities. He stated that I had four responsibilities to adhere to and then proceeded to remind me of them, as outlined below:

1. I was required to keep up my website.
2. I had to make sure that the products were available on my website, etc., to perform dropshipping.
3. I must provide customer care and support.
4. I must maintain my merchant account.

All of this was not new to me, but I guess Jacob needed to repeat it to drive home the point that my website was in a state of disarray, and something had to be done about it. Jacob continued by reminding me that my website was still under warranty, and that his team could help build and direct traffic to my website with the following methods:

- Meta Tags

- Content
- Link-building
- Search Engines
- Clean-up of codes to submit website domain
- Submissions and updates every two weeks
- Building relevance
- Changing names of photos (too many duplicates)

The craziest part about my conversation with Jacob was when he explained how his team could send me a *training video* on how to correct the title tabs. This video would also show me how to clean up the codes and errors on my own, or I could choose to have his team do it for $1,800. And there it was! I was waiting for Jacob to cut to the chase. It was all about the dollars; nothing else mattered to Jacob.

Jacob hammered home his point by having me look at another online website, EasyClosets.com. He talked about the number of people visiting that particular website which was 6,500 per month. He continued by commenting that other sites like Home Depot and Lowes got even more visitors; about 100,000 each month. But, he added, my site could only support 3,200 visitors each month, and if 10% of those visitors were to make a purchase on my website, I could potentially acquire about 3,200 sales each month.

Before Jacob could utter another word, I abruptly interjected. First, I described my frustration with my supplier, Doba.com. I explained that Doba's wholesale prices were too high, and I that I was unable to sell any products before my website went *bust*. Secondly, I reminded him that it was not my doing when the switch was made from *Embark Hosting* to *Elite Hosting*, and not my fault when my blogs didn't transfer over as a result. Thirdly, I complained that I didn't get an immediate response from the Builder Support Team during and after the switch (calls and emails went unanswered). Fourthly, I explained how I was unable to navigate the backend or backdoor of my website due to lack of instructions from the coaches. Lastly, I laid out the long, excruciating hours that I devoted to my website; loading products into categories and subcategories, assigning prices, etc., before my site went bust, and how it was all for nothing. So, no, I was not about to pay for another service, especially to correct problems or issues that I did not cause. It didn't make any sense.

Yet, Jacob proceeded to justify the reasons for purchasing the $1,800 service. He continued on and instructed me to go to Google and type in the code W3C. Afterwards, he told me to click on "Markup Validation Service," and after doing so, seventeen errors or warnings appeared on my website. All of this was like Greek to me. I hadn't the slightest clue as to what the warnings meant. Jacob exclaimed that by July 2, 2018, those errors would become more serious and would even become "strict errors" two weeks thereafter. He was very aggressive. He wanted me to agree to pay $1,800 on that day to fix the errors on my website. I told him no repeatedly, and that his company was nothing more than a scam. I finally told him that I would be contacting my lawyer, and then I hung up the phone.

TAKING THE BULL BY THE HORNS

I was so furious with Jacob, I decided to rise up and take action. It was unbelievable. He would not take no for an answer. He pushed, and pushed, and pushed even more. I had to end that call. I could feel the tension rising within me. There was no possible way for me to fix these errors on my own and Jacob knew that. He was hoping to pull one more con. That following month, on Friday, July 6, 2018, I sent the following message to the builder support team, via email:

> "Please send me the mailing address, telephone number, and full name of the Owner/CEO for your operation as soon as possible. If you are unable to provide me with this information, please refer me to the appropriate party who can give me this information. Thanks in advance for your cooperation."

This email obviously got someone's attention right away, because I received a call from an associate whose name was Ilene. She suggested that I speak with David, but quickly explained that he was not a Senior Director. David was a Customer Support person, according to Ilene, and she was his assistant. She proceeded to set up an appointment for me to speak with David on Monday, July 9, 2018.

David called me as planned. I began by thoroughly explaining my particular situation and my overall dissatisfaction. I delineated and broke down the cost of each program and service that I had purchased from October 20, 2017, to January 11, 2018. To make sure that I accounted for every purchase, I referenced the following that was written down in my notebook:

October 20-26, 2017 (Prime Corporate Services)
$9,800 – Custom-Built Website with monthly hosting fee
$1,660 – State Entity Set-Up, LLC
$2,950 – Executive Corporate Credit Package
$3,890 – Tax Preparation Program with monthly service fee

November 10, 2017 (Doba.com dropshipping membership) $2,500
Recurring yearly membership fee of $2,500

December 18, 2017 (Mastery Pro Group) $8,495
Four Coaching Sessions – Website Marketing (Phase I)

January 11, 2018 (Mastery Pro Group) $5,995.00 (reduced cost)
Fourteen Coaching Sessions – Website Marketing (Phase II)

The grand total came to $35,290.

I also talked to David about my FICO Score. I explained that my FICO Score was 803 before I bought into their business and plummeted to 711 by July 2018. I quickly pointed out that the drop in my FICO score was not the result of any late payments or missed payments on my credit cards. I always paid the minimum amount due, and I always paid on time. The drop in my FICO score was the result of having too much credit card debt, overall. I further explained how Jacob was very persistent and insistent upon me purchasing another service to fix errors on my website; errors that I did not create in the first place.

After David listened to everything that I needed to get off my chest, he stated that he would negotiate a refund on my behalf from Prime Corporate Services, Doba.com, and Mastery Pro Group. He even said that I could call his office at any time to check on his progress. Overall, I felt really good about my conversation with David because he was willing to put something in motion instead of giving me excuses.

I waited, and waited, but still no word from David. Finally, on Friday, July 27, 2018, I decided to call David's office to check on his progress, but he was not available. Ilene was not available either. The receptionist placed me on hold for a few minutes, and when she returned, she stated that I would need to speak with someone in their Resolution Department. She proceeded to set up my appointment for Monday, July 30, 2018, at 10 a.m., and she stated that David would more than likely be the person calling me on that day. I entered this date into my calendar. "Cool," I thought to myself.

July 30th came, and Ilene called to say that David was tied up, and that he would call me around 11 a.m. instead. David finally called me at 11:42 a.m. The first thing that David said was that he was unable to get me a refund from the owners. I made a plea as to why I deserved a refund and how I believed that their entire program was a scam. I insisted that David give me the address to their corporate office, the name of the owner, and the telephone number associated with their corporation. *I could feel the tension building within me.* David agreed to give me the address to their corporate office, located in Murray, Utah. But he stated that, by law, he couldn't provide me with the phone number nor the name of the owner. "What?" I asked. He reiterated that it would be illegal for him to provide that information.

He told me to try on my own to get Web Market Services to agree to a refund, and that he would, once again, try to get the other services to refund my money. He told me to work on the "back end" or seek a refund from the first program that I purchased back in October of 2017, and that he would work on the "front end, going back." Additionally, David told me to write a letter and send it to their corporate office, and that the greeting should read, "To Whom It May Concern." He explained that a gatekeeper will be the one opening up the mail and if it's "imperative enough," the gatekeeper will pass it onto the owner. David assured me that my letter would be imperative enough to get passed onto the owner. I had never heard of such foolishness before.

David asked me how much of a refund was I seeking from Web Market Services, and I told him that I would be requesting a full refund. I didn't believe that they would willingly give me a full refund, but it was a starting point. I immediately began preparing my letter to Web Market Services on July 30, 2018, after speaking with David. After I was satisfied with everything that I wanted to convey in my letter, as shown below, I sent it the following day, via certified mail.

WEB MARKET SERVICES
Murray, Utah 84117

July 30, 2018
To Whom It May Concern,

I am writing this letter to request a refund from Web Market Services. I began the program on October of 2017 and since that time, my FICO Score has plummeted. In October 2017 when I enrolled into Web Market Services, my FICO Score was 806. Today, my FICO score is 719. I can't tell you how upsetting this is for me. When I enrolled in the program on October 20, 2017, there was no mention of other services or products that I would be expected to purchase beyond what was initially discussed on that date. The services and fees that were initially discussed on October 20th included the following:

$9,800 for website through Web Market Services (premium custom built website, optimize site content and design; Embark Web Building with shopping cart, SEO friendly; $39.95 per month hosting/membership fee waived for the first 90 days; Kick Fire Gold Marketing Package; 6 months technical support; Lister Labs eBay Software for eBay auctions; eBay Professional Research Software for in-depth eBay product research; unlimited access to e-library videos, and live webinars from industry experts)

$1,660 for entity setup, instate Nevada LLC service, through Prime Corporate Services
$2,950 for Executive Corporate Credit Package, through Prime Corporate Services

The services outlined above were the only three services talked about during my initial discussion with Mitch Reynolds. I was led to believe that these were the only services that had a dollar amount attached to them. No other services or fees were discussed during my initial contact. Shortly after October 20th, I received phone calls about additional services which I had to purchase, and they included the following:

$3,890 on October 26, 2017, for a Tax Preparation Program through Prime Corporate Services, Tax Sentry, monthly service fee in the amount of $34.95

$2,500 on November 10, 2017, for DOBA dropshipping membership (cost for one year)

$8,495 on December 18, 2017, through Mastery Pro Group for website marketing and four coaching sessions with Kevin (was told that this price included four free sessions, but they were never rendered by Mastery Pro Group)

$5,995 on January 11, 2018, through Mastery Pro Group for 14 marketing coaching sessions

When I had the telephone conversation with Caleb on January 11, 2018, during the time I purchased the 14 marketing sessions, I was extremely upset. When I purchased the four sessions on December 18, 2017, with the promise of four free sessions that never occurred, I knew then that something was wrong and that caused me to worry. At that point, I had lost all credibility with the program and services. It felt as if I was being swindled or scammed. I became nervous during that phone call, started sweating and crying, and then my heart started racing. I had difficulty sleeping from worry over the next few nights and then on January 14, 2018, I had a heart attack. I was admitted to the hospital and had to undergo treatment. I now have to take four different medications because of that heart attack.

Month after month, from the initial start of the program up to the point when I purchased the 14 marketing sessions, I watched my credit score plummet, as stated earlier. I have enclosed a copy of a chart from my Discover Card Services showing the drop in my credit score. It's very troublesome.

I tried diligently after my release from the hospital to think differently and to remain calm. But during the months of March and April of this year, that all changed when my website was relocated from Embark to Elite. This change caused me nothing but stress because my Elite website had missing items/products and all my blog posts and pictures were missing. I became so frustrated; my stress level began to rise again. As a result, I placed a temporary hold on my marketing sessions with Kevin on May 2, 2018. I needed to break away from this turmoil. I also did this because I didn't want to risk having another heart attack.

The final straw was on June 22, 2018, when I received a phone call from Jacob. I noticed that he had left several messages on my answering machine beforehand. On June 22nd, Jacob tried to sell me another service and he stated that it would cost $1,800. He indicated that I had some warning errors on my website and that it would cost me $1,800 to have them fixed by their team. He said that I had 17 error codes as of June 22nd and that they would only get worse by July 2, 2018. This really angered me, and I started to feel my heart racing. I also started sweating. I knew I had to calm down because, again, I did not want to risk having another heart attack. I told Jacob that I was NOT going to buy any more services.

I can't begin to tell you how upsetting this entire experience has been for me. I have never experienced this type of stress before. I need to finally end the madness and take back my life because I feel trapped in a money pit. I have spoken with David on two different occasions. I first spoke with him on July 9th to express my dissatisfaction and to request a refund. **To date, I have invested $35,290**. He said that he would present my case to the owners and try to get my money refunded. When I spoke with him again earlier today, July 30, 2017, he told me that he was not successful at convincing Web Market Services to refund my money. The other owners, according to David, were willing to refund my money but decided against it when they learned that Web Market Services refused to do the same. This is very disturbing.

I consider myself to be a fair and honest person. I work hard and I treat others the way that I would want to be treated. I am also a trusting person. When I received the initial phone calls from Web Market Services and Prime Corporate Services, I felt as if the individuals on the other end of the phone were people that I could trust. I guess I was wrong because there was no mention of additional services that I would need to purchase beyond what I initially purchased on October 20, 2017. Looking back, it all seemed like a trap in that in order to advance, I had to continue to dish out more and more money to get to that next level. It is simply unfair and deceitful for a company to not lay all the cards on the table at the very beginning. I am requesting a refund because **$35,290** in credit card debt is a serious matter and I know that if I had been provided with all the details regarding the *services and fees for the entire program, I never would have signed a contract with Web Market Services. I am hoping that you are a man of honor.* **Please do the right thing and grant me a refund.**

*Sincerely,
Bridget R. Knight*

As you can tell from this letter, I was pretty angry and desperate. I was hoping that the owner would understand my position and have some remorse. I knew it would be a long shot, but I was holding onto every possibility. With each passing day, the angrier I became. I guess writing the letter and putting everything into perspective left me with a feeling of disgust. I was disgusted with myself for falling for the con. I was disgusted with myself for not recognizing the signs that were right in front of me. *"What was wrong with me?"*

ANOTHER SUFFERED HEART ATTACK

Again, the worry and shame became too much for me to bear. I suffered another mild heart attack on August 8, 2018, and just as before on January 14, 2018, I was hospitalized with the same diagnosis. I had to undergo the same treatments as before. Thankfully, there was no damage to my heart. I was lucky to have survived another heart attack, but I still had unresolved issues with my ecommerce business. During my hospitalization on August 8-9, 2018, I received several voice messages on my cell phone from two representatives with Mastery Pro Group, named Brendon and Carla. I was unable to take their calls because the doctors and nurses were attending to me or treating me during those times. As soon as I was available, I returned Carla's phone call but could only speak with her briefly. I explained what was happening and told her that I wouldn't be able to speak to her nor Brendon at length until after my release from the hospital.

Fortunately, I was released on August 9, 2018, and made plans to call both Carla and Brendon the following day. Carla wasn't available when I called her on August 10th, but she stated that she would return my call later that afternoon at around 1 p.m. During the interim, I received a phone call from Brendon and was able to speak with him at length from, 11:44 a.m. to 12:15 p.m. I talked to him about my overall disappointment with my business and I reiterated what I had already stated in my letter to the owner. I told Brendon that I wanted a refund. I concluded our conversation by insisting that my website be taken down and that the hosting fees be terminated. Brendon said he would work on getting that done.

I waited for Carla to call me back at 1 p.m., but instead of her returning my phone call, I received a call from Jeff, with Mastery Pro Group. I was sounding like a broken record by this time. Again, I expressed my dissatisfaction with their business products and services, and the overall financial strain that the business had caused me. When Jeff asked me what amount I was seeking, I replied by asking for a full refund. He stated that a full refund would be highly unlikely. I then requested a 50% refund. As we were concluding our conversation, Jeff assured me that he would talk to the owners and then follow-up with me on Monday, August 13, 2018, at around 1 p.m. to discuss a resolution. I was beginning to think that I was getting the run-around treatment.

Monday, August 13, 2018, approached. I waited and waited for Jeff to call around 1 p.m. but received *nothing*. It wasn't until two hours later that I received a phone call. Instead of Jeff, it was a receptionist asking me to reschedule my appointment with Jeff. Our new appointment was now set for August 15th at 4 p.m. I thought to myself and exclaimed, "Here we go again! Will there ever be a fair resolution, if any at all?"

CHAPTER FOUR
THE RESOLUTION

I honestly didn't think that Jeff would follow up with me on August 15, 2018, to discuss a resolution. I thought for sure that he would either blow me off or reschedule our appointment. I was not counting on him to call, but to my surprise, he called me around the same time and date that he promised. And again, to my surprise, he was prepared to discuss an actual resolution that was offered to me by Mastery Pro Group. When Jeff was describing the refund amounts that I would receive for my four coaching sessions, and then for the fourteen coaching sessions, I began shaking my head from side-to-side. "Unbelievable," I thought. "My gut instinct was right! There was never going to be a fair resolution."

    For the four coaching sessions, Mastery Pro Group was only willing to refund 20% of $8,495 ($1,699 to be credited back to my credit card). For the fourteen coaching sessions, Mastery Pro Group was only willing to refund 15% of $5,995 ($899.25 to be credited back to my credit card). I was in a tight spot. Should I accept this offer, or should I fight for more? Jeff had already stated that this was Mastery Pro Group's best offer, but was he really being truthful? I was in such a predicament.

Given the position I was in and reaching a conclusion that "something was better than nothing," I accepted the offer. Jeff sent me the "Master Services Group Settlement and Release Agreement" for each of the two coaching programs, via email, and I signed them accordingly. Shortly thereafter, the refund amounts were credited back to my credit card. Even though I got far less than what I had hoped to get from Mastery Pro Group, I was glad that that particular hurdle was finally over. Next stop – Web Marketing Services.

I needed to first follow-up with David, so I planned to call him that following Monday, August 20, 2018. I was chugging right along. Keep in mind that David was the associate who gave me the address to their corporate office but couldn't provide me with the owner's name and telephone number. He stated back in July that he would try to get Web Marketing Services to agree to a refund. Before I had a chance to call David, however, I received a phone call from Wendell, an associate within the Resolution Department. He wanted to know how things were progressing with the other owners. I complained to him about the low refunds that I received from Mastery Pro Group, but I told him I was thankful, nonetheless. Wendell suggested that I stick with my plan to call and follow-up with David. Wendell then told me to call him back after speaking with David, but to not let David know this. Wendell simply said that he wanted to know what David and I talked about. I agreed, but asked myself, "What? Why was Wendell being so secretive? Why didn't Wendell want David to know that I was planning to call him (Wendell) back? Was Wendell hiding something?" None of this made sense.

As planned, I spoke with David on August 20, 2018. From the moment we started talking, I could tell that David seemed upset or disappointed. I asked him what was going on, but he wouldn't say at first. A few seconds later, David said, "Mastery Pro Group told me that you were upset with me, and that I was unprofessional."

I quickly replied, "What?" Where was all this coming from? I assured David that there was absolutely no truth to that statement. I reiterated this over and over again. I needed David to believe that I hadn't said anything negative about him and that Mastery Pro Group was simply lying. Fortunately, David believed me. He said that he would continue to "go to bat" for me to get the refunds that I deserved. I was so relieved to hear that. Our phone conversation ended on a positive note.

Did Mastery Pro Group purposely lie to David about how I felt about him? What was their end game? Was it to discourage David from working on my behalf to get the refunds I requested from the other companies? Was it to cause resentment or create a huge rift between David and me? What was Wendell's motive?

I never did discover the real reason as to why David was lied to by Mastery Pro Group, but I had a strong suspicion about Wendell. I believed Wendell deliberately set me up. I didn't have any proof, but it all started to make sense the next morning. How disturbing and petty. My phone calls to the Resolution Department from that day forward all went unanswered. Over the next few months, I tried repeatedly to get the refunds I requested from the other partners, but my requests simply "fell on deaf ears." I was completely ignored.

It was apparent that no other refunds would be issued, so I concentrated on my plans to build my retirement home in Belize, Central America. I sold my primary residence in October of 2018, and moved in with my cousin in the Summerlin community of Las Vegas, while awaiting the construction of my home in Belize. It would take about a year to complete. I packed up all the documents pertaining to my ecommerce business and placed everything in storage, along with my furniture. I was embarking on a new life in paradise. I was thrilled! Since I had a lot of equity in my house when I sold it, I used some of the proceeds from the sale to pay off all the credit card debt that I accumulated from my ecommerce business. I had to finally admit to myself that I tried and failed, and it was time to move on. I dissolved my LLC (BTK Unlimited Concepts) and simply refocused my attention on my future plans in Belize.

LAST DITCH EFFORT

While living with my cousin in the Summerlin community, I was able to regroup and concentrate on reclaiming my life and getting things back on the right track. However, it just seemed as if my failed ecommerce business kept rearing its ugly head. When I was out shopping one day, I received a voice message and email from Doba.com (dropshipping), reminding me that my yearly membership fee would automatically charge to my credit card that they had on file, but at the regular yearly rate. Remember, I paid $2,500 to Doba in November of 2017 for a one-year membership, but the regular yearly rate was $4,000. I immediately called Doba's customer service representative and told her that I had dissolved my ecommerce business and that I was officially canceling my membership with Doba.com on that day. I actually thought that I had already canceled my membership back in 2018, and I had no idea that a yearly membership fee would be charged to my credit card automatically. That information had not been disclosed to me. Nevertheless, I was just thankful that I received prior notice from Doba.com before the recurring membership fee was actually charged to my credit card. It was definitely a "hallelujah moment!" I dodged another bullet! I refocused my attention on Belize and worked diligently with my builder to finalize the plans for my retirement home. He and his architects did an awesome job of designing my beautiful home, inside and out.

Sadly, the beautiful house that I had intended to build in Belize did not happen, due to unexpected reasons beyond my control. This forced me to quickly change my plans. And then, COVID happened! The COVID-19 pandemic began shortly after I managed to purchase and move into another house in Las Vegas.

More specific, I vacated my cousin's house and moved into a modest size townhouse that I had purchased in August of 2019. It needed some upgrading, so I spent some time making minor improvements before officially moving in one day before Thanksgiving. A few months later, the Coronavirus was upon us. This was a very scary time because of so many unknowns about the virus back then. Being indoors most of the time (because the virus was so deadly) caused me to reflect on my ecommerce business and to hate myself for not pushing harder to get more refunds. After giving it some more thought, I decided to unpack the storage box which contained all the documents from my ecommerce business. I wanted to give it one last shot. *After all – what did I have to lose?*

Without any further delay, I composed and mailed the following letter to Web Market Services, requesting a refund for the amount I paid for my website.

WEB MARKET SERVICES
Murray, Utah 84117
RE: Unresolved Complaint and Refund Request

July 21, 2020
Dear Sir/Madam,

I am writing this letter in the hopes of resolving a matter that began in October of 2017 and which I tried unsuccessfully to resolve during the months of July and August of 2018. I hope you can have someone contact me to finally resolve my issue as outlined below.

To begin with, I entered into an agreement with Web Market Services on October 10, 2017, in the amount of $9,800 for the purposes of building a website and other related services. I have enclosed a copy of the paid invoice. For the record, this is the second letter that I have written to Web Market Services in the hopes of reaching a resolution. I had several conversations with several individuals during July and August of 2018 from the Resolution Department, but the matter regarding the Website Service Package that I initially purchased on October 10, 2017, was never resolved. I requested a partial refund for the website service, but I kept getting the run-around and promises of follow-up phone calls that never happened. I stopped receiving phone calls from the resolution department altogether after August of 2018. In early October of 2018, I sold my primary residence, so my land line number was no longer in service. My cellular number, however, was still active and I made this known. The initial letter that I sent to Web Market Services was dated July 30, 2018, and it clearly outlined my complaints and the reasons why I felt I deserved a partial refund.

After a lot of back-and-forth discussions with the Resolutions Department, I received a 20% refund for the Website Marketing and four coaching sessions because the additional four free coaching sessions were never rendered by Mastery Pro Group. I also received a 15% refund for 14 Marketing coaching sessions because I never completed these sessions. These refunds were arranged/completed on August 15, 2018, and were greatly appreciated. In the initial letter that I sent dated July 30, 2018, I described the stress, hospitalizations, and other health-related problems that I had experienced with the issues surrounding my website. These were the reasons why I needed to terminate my agreements with Web Market Services, Prime Corporate Services, and Mastery Pro Group. I was trying to avoid another heart attack and hospitalization.

I suffered a great deal of loss in terms of the time, money, energy, and research devoted to managing my website, especially when there was a sudden shift/relocation from Embark Web Building to Elite. When this relocation happened, all of my blogs and pictures were completely lost. There were tons and tons of errors that were not addressed or fixed by Web Market Services, even though I tried unsuccessfully to gain technical support. My requests went unanswered. The time that I spent writing my personal blogs, taking photos, uploading photos, doing research, and organizing/categorizing my dropship products via Doba, was completely wasted when the relocation occurred. It was a shift that I never saw coming because I was never notified beforehand. When I signed the initial agreement for the Platinum Custom Built Embark Website, technical support was included in this package. My website was down for several days or at least a week when the relocation occurred. I tried unsuccessfully to secure technical support after putting in numerous requests. These were some of the arguments that I made when I spoke with individuals within the resolution department back in July and August of 2018 (David, Ilene, Brendon, Carla, Jeff, Wendell, to name a few).

After carefully examining my notes, I believe that the last phone call that I received from the Resolution Department was on August 20, 2018. I spoke with David at around 8:30 a.m. on that date and he wanted me to know how things were progressing with my refund. He assured me that he would try his best to get the refund that I deserved. Unfortunately, I never received any more phone calls after that date. If David had tried to contact me on my land line after October 4, 2018, he would not have been able to complete the call. As stated earlier, I sold my home in early October of 2018. My cellular phone, however, was still active. My records/files had been in storage up until the time I recently moved to my current location. These files contained anecdotal notes/records and documents related to my ecommerce business with Mastery Pro Group and Web Market Services. I felt it necessary to write once again to explain my position and to request a partial refund for the uncontrollable changes to my website and the losses that I suffered as a result.

I would like to speak directly with someone from your Resolution Department to finally clear up this matter and to discuss the amount of my refund. I can be reached any day of the week between the hours of 8 a.m. and 4:30 p.m. Pacific Time. Thank you in advance for your cooperation and I look forward to someone reaching out to me.

Sincerely,
Bridget R. Knight

I knew that there was a strong possibility that no one would follow-up with me, especially during a pandemic, but to my surprise, Wendell got in contact with me. He actually tried calling me twice, but I was tied up in traffic. I returned his call as soon as I was available on July 29, 2020, at 4:40 p.m. Wendell stated that he remembered talking to me back in 2018, and that he would try his best to get me a partial refund for my website. He offered some suggestions, one being to sell my website to another client and that he would make some inquiries. I liked this idea! Wendell said that he would get back with me by Friday, July 31, 2020.

Wendell kept his promise and followed up with me on July 31st at 12:08 p.m. He stated that a client offered $1,500 for my website. He further stated that a second offer from another client may be on the table, but that it hadn't been confirmed yet. Wendell went on to explain that if I was to accept the offer, I would simply sign a standard document and the client would then send Web Market Services a check in the agreed-upon amount. Afterwards, Web Corporate Services would issue a cashier's check to me for that amount, via U.S. mail. He added that they would have to confirm that the client had the available funds to make the purchase. Afterwards, he explained that it would take approximately twenty-four to forty-eight hours to cut the check. Lastly, the check would be mailed to my home address immediately afterwards. I told Wendell that I wanted to wait for the second offer. After all, I paid $9,800 for my custom-built website when I first bought into the business back in October of 2017. Fifteen hundred dollars was a long way from that amount. Wendell said that he would follow-up with news about the second offer on August 3rd or August 4th.

On Tuesday morning, August 4, 2020, Wendell followed up, as he had indicated. We talked for approximately five minutes about the second offer that was made for my website, which was $2,000. I was hoping for at least $5,000 but I somehow knew that haggling would be a losing battle, so I accepted the offer. Something was better than nothing.

I signed the appropriate document electronically, and after it was all said and done, I received a cashier's check in the amount of $2,000 from Web Market Services on August 12, 2020. I quickly deposited my check and called Wendell to thank him for his support. It was a long time coming but I was relieved that this chapter in my life had finally come to an end; or at least I thought it had ended. It was just about to rear its ugly head once again and I never saw it coming.

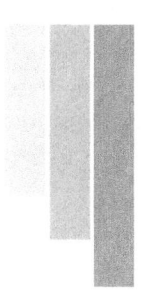

CHAPTER FIVE
THE REVELATION

A vaccine for COVID-19 was discovered rather quickly, so when it was my time to get vaccinated, I made an appointment and celebrated privately after getting my shot. It was a glorious feeling! I felt empowered and eager to finally build my retirement home. The townhouse that I was currently living in was not my ideal of retirement living, and plus, I knew that I wouldn't be living there for long. Furthermore, it was evident that the house that I had dreamed of building in Belize was never going to happen, so I set my sites on other properties outside of Las Vegas, but not too far from the city. I finally decided on a location during the latter part of 2020, and I entered into an agreement to purchase a newly built home in March of 2021, in Logandale, NV. It took about six months to construct due to the pandemic and supply shortages. The months went by rather quickly, however. In October of 2021, I closed escrow on my townhouse in Las Vegas and the house in Logandale, and finally moved into my new home shortly thereafter.

Logandale, NV is approximately sixty miles north of Las Vegas. It is a small, quiet community not far from Mesquite which is home to nine different golf courses. I love my small-town community and my neighbors are all so friendly. It is a great place to retire and St. George, Utah is only a short, one-hour drive away. St. George has more businesses and big-box stores than Logandale and Mesquite. So, when I need to shop at major stores or dine in certain restaurants, for instance, I can either drive to nearby St. George or to Las Vegas.

St. George is a beautiful city, but when I occasionally think of Utah, I think about my failed ecommerce business, because Web Market Services, Prime Corporate Services, and Mastery Pro Group were incorporated or based in Utah. Those feelings never truly go away, but I try to suppress my emotions and replace them with positive thoughts. On one particular day, however, the memory of that time came rushing back to my mind: front and center. It occurred on the same day that I was entertaining my Canadian friends (a married couple) who had driven out from Las Vegas to see my new home. They were once my next door neighbors when I was living in my townhouse in Las Vegas; the townhouse I sold. Anyhow, my neighbors are snowbirds, and they usually spend six months in Las Vegas during the winter, and six months in Quebec, Canada during the summer. So, when I was entertaining my friends that particular afternoon on Monday, March 7, 2022, I received a phone call from Homeland Security Investigations, in the Southern District of New York. Normally, I don't answer my cell phone when I am entertaining guests, but I made an exception this time and I can't explain why. What I learned that afternoon would change my entire perspective about my washed-up ecommerce business.

NATIONWIDE SCAM EXPOSED

The conversation that I had with one of the special agents first began with a lot of questions pertaining to the purchase of my ecommerce, affiliate marketing business (e.g., purchase dates, types of products and services purchased, the cost for each, timelines, people I had contact with, the coaching sessions, etc.). The agent was gathering information during this stage. He then brought in another special agent on another line who asked me additional questions. I remember saying to myself, "Was this real or was it a joke? Was this another scam? How can I trust these individuals?"

I kept thinking that I had personally done something wrong, but when I learned that they were investigating and building a case against the individuals who sold me the products and services, I sighed a big sigh of relief. It all made sense now and it confirmed what I had suspected from the very beginning! The ecommerce business that I purchased through Web Market Services, Prime Corporate Services, and Mastery Pro Group was a nationwide SCAM! The special agents informed me that there were several defendants who had already been charged, and had pled guilty, and were currently serving time in prison for their involvement. There were still others facing charges and the agents asked for my assistance with building a stronger case against those individuals. *I agreed.*

At this point, I had no idea of who Jennifer Shah was or what role she played in this nationwide telemarketing scam. The agents asked me to gather and send them all the information and documents that I still had in my possession. Fortunately for them, I kept everything:

- Every email message saved
- Every phone call documented
- Every purchase agreement saved
- Every credit card invoice showing all purchases
- Every coaching session documented
- Every homework assignment that was given and completed
- Every letter I mailed
- Every activity that was given

- Every contact made with coaches, etc.
- Every conversation documented, with dates and times
- Every handwritten note
- Every item sold on eBay documented

They seemed ecstatic that I still had all of these items in my possession. I explained that my three ring notebook that housed my documents was about three inches thick, and was well organized by events, and placed in chronological order. They asked if I could send copies of my documents to them. Without hesitation, I said, "YES!" One of the agents stated that he would send me an email, containing their names and address, and a brief description of what we discussed. I assured them that I would start pulling everything together and make plans to mail the documents before Friday, March 11, 2022. Without delay, I got right to work the following day. It was an exhausting task because of the volume of information that I had to scan or copy. Nevertheless, I was able to meet my target date by sending my documents, via priority mail, to the special agents at Homeland Security Investigations in New York, NY. The package was due to arrive on March 11, 2022, but it would take additional time before finally making its way to the special agents' office. On March 24, 2022, I received an email from one of the special agents confirming the receipt of my documents. Hallelujah!

NEXT STEPS

About two months later, I received an email from Kelsey, a female special agent, who explained the next order of business. She wanted to know if I could meet with her and an assistant U.S. attorney, via a "Web-Ex" online meeting, Friday, June 10, 2022, at 9 a.m. The purpose of that meeting was to go over the documents that I submitted and to discuss next expectations. I agreed. This was our first official meeting. I was nervous at first, but the more we talked, the less nervous I became. There was a lot of information revealed about the business that I bought into. The level of fraud ran very deep; a lot deeper than I had originally suspected. I was actually flabbergasted and in disbelief. This fraud had been occurring for nearly a decade. I knew it was a scam early on, but I didn't have the means, method, or the money to fight such as powerful entity on my own. There were more than ten individuals perpetrating this fraud. I knew I had to get involved and be one of the forces to help extinguish this con game. By the time our meeting was over, I felt even more empowered and eager to assist the attorney and special agents with their investigation in any way, shape, or form. Still, at this point, I had no idea of who Jennifer Shah was or what role she played in this nationwide telemarketing scam.

CHAPTER SIX
THE U.S. V. JENNIFER SHAH

My next meeting with the assistant U.S. attorney and special agent, Kelsey, would occur on Wednesday, June 22, 2022. It would be a true face-to-face meeting. During the interim, I flew to Monterey, CA to visit my nephew and meet up with other family members. We had gathered together to welcome a new addition to the family – my nephew's first child, a baby boy. I was in Monterey for six fun-filled days. It was a pleasant, exhilarating break! During the times that I spent sitting and relaxing in my hotel room, I occasionally thought about my upcoming meeting with the attorney and special agent, and wondered if I could actually make a profound difference in their case.

Upon returning home to Mesquite, NV on Monday, June 20, 2022, I became more and more enthusiastic about meeting with the attorney and special agent. I was ready, willing, and able to help them with their case. My mind was made up. There was no turning back for me. Our meeting date was confirmed for Wednesday,

June 22, 2022, at 9:30 a.m. The meeting was due to take place in one of the offices inside a government building in Las Vegas, NV. I was familiar with the area.

Thankfully, I didn't have to drive myself to Las Vegas, which was refreshing. I was extremely exhausted from my Monterey trip, so the special agent arranged for a driver to pick me up. The attorney and Kelsey had flown into Las Vegas one or two days beforehand, so I imagined they were well-rested and eager to get started. We all arrived at the government building around the same time. An office clerk immediately checked us into an office where we concentrated and poured through the evidence that I sent to them back in March.

It was right at this point when I saw the name *Jennifer Shah* for the first time. Her name was on the label of a three-ring black binder that the attorney had given me, but I had no prior knowledge of who she was. I didn't even think to ask. I only knew that she was the defendant in the case and that she was facing fraud charges. I didn't know all the details about the case, only the bare minimum. But I suspected that Jennifer was the owner or CEO of Mastery Pro Group, the company that sold me the very expensive coaching sessions. Again, I didn't even think to ask.

During the bulk of the day, the attorney, Kelsey, and I poured through all my evidence that was contained in that three-ring black binder. They each had a similar binder with duplicate information. The attorney and Kelsey commented on how well-organized my documents were displayed and delivered to them back in March. I had divided my documents into eight sections, and each section began with a summary or outline, detailing the enclosures for that particular section. I included all documents that I felt were pertinent to my ecommerce business and helpful to their case. I left "no stone unturned". I take great pride in my organizational skills and how things are presented or displayed and have done so practically my entire life.

The attorney and Kelsey went on to state that I had pretty much done most of their work for them, in terms of how my documents were organized. Collectively, the documents that I submitted to them as evidence was just a small representation of the facts. The "meat and potatoes" of the evidence were housed in my personal three-ring pink binder (the one that's about three inches thick). I brought this binder to the meeting with me and was prepared to offer any supportive information or additional evidence that could further help them in their case against Jennifer Shah.

Still, I had no clue as to who Jennifer Shah was. My black binder was labeled, *"The U.S. v. Jennifer Shah,"* along with her case number, followed by my name printed underneath. Yet, I didn't bother to ask either of them about Jennifer Shah nor did I think to Google her name during our lunch break. Again, I just assumed that Jennifer was one of the owners or CEO of the entity that I purchased my ecommerce business from. I began to wonder, was Jennifer Shah the person whom David would not disclose when I requested the CEO's or owner's name back in 2018? Why was it illegal for David to disclose her name to me, as he so quickly pointed out?

As we were scrutinizing my documents with a "fine-tooth comb," and approached the section where I asked David for the CEO's or owner's name, the attorney stated that there was no law prohibiting David from giving me that information. David had obviously withheld the CEO'S name or owner's name on purpose. What possessed David to lie? What was he trying to cover up? Still, I didn't ask a single question about Jennifer Shah even though her name was printed in big, bold letters on the cover of my binder.

After going through all the evidence in my binder, we talked about the trial date, the trial procedures, and expectations. I was informed that the trial would be held in New York City, and that I should keep July 17th – 23rd open for travel and the actual trial. The trial was expected to begin July 18, 2022. The attorney wanted me to be the first witness to testify. The pressure began to build inside me, but I quickly regained my composure and concurred. I wanted nothing more than to help the prosecution win their case. I wanted justice, not only for myself but for the other victims as well. I was prepared to do whatever it would take.

As we were about to wrap things up for the day and make our departure, Kelsey stated that she would contact me at a later time to go over all the particulars and complexities about the trial process, and what I should expect leading up to the trial date. I was truly looking forward to our next conversation. We departed the building at around 3:30 p.m. and the driver returned me home safely by 5:00 p.m. *I thought to myself – my testimony could really make a difference in the outcome of Jennifer Shah's trial. There seems to be a lot riding on my testimony, so I definitely need to be on my "A Game".*

GLORIOUS DAYS AHEAD

The excitement was building! Special Agent Kelsey called me a few days later, as promised, and she brilliantly laid out and spoke in detail about the following:

- Mock trial before the actual trial
- Cross-examination and what it looks like
- Direct-examination and what it looks like
- Layout of the court room (witness box, jury, judge's bench, etc.)
- Open-ended questions
- Leading questions
- Repeating questions
- Yes/No questions
- Two-part questions
- Reframing questions
- Re-direct examination
- Re-cross examination

I was super charged and ready to testify. Someone else from Kelsey's office would be in contact with me to arrange my flight and hotel stay. I was expected to arrive in New York City on Sunday, July 17, 2022, and testify in court on Tuesday, July 19, 2022. These dates were fast approaching, so I made plans to begin packing my bags the weekend prior to my expected arrival date in

New York. My hotel and flight plans had not been finalized yet, but I figured everything would be confirmed by July 11th or 12th.

I was leaving nothing to chance. I had to cover all the bases. I packed my black binder that contained all of my evidence, as well as my own personal pink binder that contained the "meat and potatoes." I packed the appropriate outfits to wear when giving my testimony in court and the appropriate clothing for New York's weather, *including my umbrella*. I packed enough clothes for at least three days, and I made sure I had enough money to tip the bellhop, waiters, etc. It was just a matter of time, and the excitement was continuing to build. I was a week away from telling my story in court. *Still, it never occurred to me to find out about Jennifer Shah, and the role she played in the scam.*

CHAPTER SEVEN
THE PLEA DEAL

It was about one week before the trial was set to start. The pressure was on again, but it was good pressure, friendly pressure. I was not fearful. I was not hesitant. My thinking was not muddled. I welcomed the opportunity to testify and tell my story. The prosecutors definitely had a massive undertaking ahead of them, and I felt positive that the state would win their case against Jennifer. The prosecutors were seeking justice not only for me, but for the other victims as well. I had a duty to perform. There was no room for error and there was no turning back.

And then, the unexpected happened. I received an email, dated July 11, 2022, from the assistant U.S. attorney, the attorney I met with in Las Vegas. It was addressed to all parties and stated, *"Defendant Jennifer Shah is scheduled to enter a guilty plea on July 11, 2022, at 10:30 a.m., Eastern Time. If you wish to attend by telephone, please use the following dial-in and access code. Apologies for the last-minute notice, but the proceeding was unexpected and was just scheduled.*

Assuming the judge accepts Ms. Shah's guilty plea, the trial currently scheduled for July 18, 2022, will not be held." This was shocking. What had caused Jennifer Shah to change her plea? I eagerly awaited news about the plea deal from the special agent.

When I actually read the email, it was too late to dial in and listen to the proceedings at the time when Jennifer was scheduled to announce her guilty plea. This was due to the time difference. I read the attorney's email at 10 a.m., Pacific Time (my time), which was 1:00 p.m., Eastern Time (New York's time). By that time, Jennifer had already changed her plea from not guilty to guilty. So, that was that; the trial was canceled. It was actually a bitter-sweet moment for me. On one hand, I was disappointed that no one would hear my testimony and the testimony of other witnesses for the prosecution. No one would ever know the ugly, true account of what really transpired, and the pain Jennifer Shah's actions caused. No one would ever know about the real suffering. No one would ever know about the financial devastation suffered by her victims. No one would ever know about the mental and physical anguish. On the other hand, I was relieved that Jennifer had changed her plea to guilty. By admitting guilt, she was taking responsibility for her actions. Or was she? Did Jennifer have ulterior motives? Was one of her motives a reduced prison sentence? If she had not pled guilty, she would have been facing 30 – 50 years in prison, according to the charges. I guess I will never know.

But who exactly was Jennifer Shah? It was time to do some digging. It was time to dive in and uncover information about who she really was, the charges she pled guilty to, and her plea deal. So, I finally Googled her name.

It only took seconds for me to find Jennifer on social media. I was astounded by what I read. There was a massive amount of information on her. I quickly began making the following notes because I wanted to confirm most of this information with Special Agent, Kelsey.

- A TV personality

- One of the Real Housewives of Salt Lake City, Utah
- Involved in telemarketing scam spanning nearly a decade
- Arrested and formally charged in March of 2021
- Charged with one count of conspiracy to commit wire fraud, and one count of conspiracy to commit money laundering
- Defrauded hundreds of victims
- Some of her co-conspirators already serving prison terms
- Other co-conspirators facing pending charges
- Flaunted her lavish lifestyle
- Huge wardrobe consisting of expensive designer outfits, shoes, and handbags
- Expensive jewelry and accessories
- Married to a football coach
- Bragged about making millions of dollars through her business
- Two children
- Ordered to pay the government $6,500,000
- Ordered to pay restitution to victims in the amount of $9,500,000
- Targeted mostly vulnerable people and those 55 and over
- Facing 10-14 years in prison (plea)
- Her legal woes? Really?

I read article-after-article on social media and looked at loads of pictures and videos. For me, it was startling and hard to digest. It was a bit overwhelming to say the least. What kept going through my mind was the notion that a TV celebrity had caused so much devastation for nearly a decade. *Why? What was the driving force? Why did Jennifer do what she did?*

I talked to Special Agent Kelsey about two days later, and she confirmed the answers to all my questions. She and the assistant attorney could not previously disclose the details to me about

Jennifer Shah due to various reasons that could have compromised their case. I fully understood their reasoning. Had I known about Jennifer Shah before the expected trial date, I would have been shaken or distressed ahead of testifying in court. I would have had difficulty maintaining my composure. I would have been "off balanced." So, all-in-all, it was a good call on their part to not disclose. Nevertheless, I had every opportunity to Google or research Jennifer's background prior to the date of her plea deal, but I chose not to bother.

The more I read about Jennifer Shah, the more disgusted I became. How could a mother of two, who has a husband earning a hefty salary as a football coach, defraud innocent, hardworking elderly people? *How could Jennifer Shah continue to defraud her victims over and over again, draining them dry, financially?* Only Jennifer can answer this question. Regardless of her answers, I believe that Jennifer knew exactly what she was doing, so there is no justification for her actions. She didn't appear to have or show any remorse. The mere fact that she actually tried to cover up the fraud purports the notion that she was fully aware, yet continued to perpetrate the fraud until she was caught. Fraud is fraud.

I continued to dig even deeper online and was able to locate a copy of the grand jury charges that were filed against her and one of her associates. I was amazed by what I discovered, but not at all surprised by the elaborate scheme that Jennifer and her associates orchestrated, particularly S.S., Jennifer's first assistant. The following legal document, as prepared by the US attorney of the southern district of New York, highlights portions of their scheme:

The United States of America – v – Jennifer Shah, and S.S., Defendants
COUNT ONE
(Conspiracy to Commit Fraud)

OVERVIEW OF THE SCHEME
1. *"From at least in or about 2012 until at least in or about March 2021, in the Southern District of New York and*

elsewhere, Jennifer Shah and S.S., the defendants, together with others known and unknown (collectively, the 'Participants') carried out a wide-ranging telemarketing scheme that defrauded hundreds of victims (the 'Victims') throughout the U.S., many of whom were over age 55, by selling those Victims so-called 'business services' in connection with the Victim's purported online businesses (the 'Business Opportunity Scheme')."

2. "In order to perpetrate the Business Opportunity Scheme, Participants, including Jennifer Shah and S.S., the defendants, engaged in a widespread, coordinated effort to traffic in **lists** of potential victims, or **'leads,'** many of whom had previously made an initial investment to create an online business with other Participants in the Scheme. Leads were initially generated by sales floors operating in, among other places, Arizona, Nevada and Utah. The owners and operators of those sales floors operated in coordination with several telemarketing sales floors in the New York and New Jersey area, including in Manhattan, and provided lead lists and assistance in fighting Victim refund requests to other Participants operating those floors."

3. "Jennifer Shah and S.S., the defendants, among other things, generated and sold leads to other Participants for use by their telemarketing sales floors with the knowledge that the individuals they had identified as 'leads' would be defrauded by the other Participants. J.Shah and S.S. yielded a share of the fraudulent revenue per the terms of their agreement with those Participants ..."

4. "To perpetrate the Business Opportunity Scheme, certain of the Participants sold alleged services purporting to make the management of Victims' businesses more efficient or profitable, including Tax Preparation or Website Design Services, notwithstanding that many Victims were elderly and did not own a computer. At the outset of the Business Opportunity Scheme, certain Participants employed by a purported fulfillment company, sent a given Victim electronic

or paper pamphlets or provided so-called '<u>coaching sessions</u>' regarding these purported online businesses, but at no point did the defendants intend that the Victims would actually earn any of the promised return on their intended investment, nor did the Victims earn any such returns."

5. "Jennifer Shah and S.S., the defendants, undertook significant efforts to <u>conceal</u> their roles in the Business Opportunity Scheme. For example, J.Shah and S.S., among other things, <u>incorporated their Business Entities</u> using third parties' names and instructed other Participants to do the same, used and directed others to use encrypted messaging applications to communicate with other Participants, instructed other Participants to send J.Shah's and S.S's share of certain fraud proceeds to offshore bank accounts, and made numerous cash withdrawals structured to avoid currency transaction reporting requirements."

<u>STATUTORY ALLEGATIONS</u>

6. "From at least in or about 2012 up to and including at least in or about March 2021, ... Jennifer Shah and S.S., the defendants, and others known and unknown, willfully and knowingly, did combine, conspire, confederate, and agree together and with each other to commit wire fraud in connection with the conduct of telemarketing..."

7. "It was a part and an object of the conspiracy that Jennifer Shah and S.S., the defendants, and others, willfully and knowingly, having devised and intending to devise a scheme and artifice to defraud, and for obtaining money and property by means of false and fraudulent pretenses, representations, and promises, would and did transmit and cause to be transmitted by means of wire communication in interstate and foreign commerce, writings, signs, signals, pictures, and sounds for the purpose of executing such scheme and artifice. J.Shah, S.S. and others induced and caused Victims to pay thousands of dollars to obtain so-called '<u>coaching</u>' and

'*business services,*' *which they represented would make the management of the Victims' purported online businesses more efficient and/or profitable, when, in actuality, the 'services' would provide little or no value to the Victims' businesses, which were essentially nonexistent.*"

Count two, conspiracy to commit money laundering, was also delineated in this document, but I only skimmed through the main points of this charge and made some mental notes. This money laundering charge was equally disturbing, but the charge was dropped, per the plea bargain. The full document outlining both charges is available online.

So, now that I knew what the charges entailed, what did Jennifer's plea bargain consist of exactly? I continued to poke deeper and soon located a copy of the plea bargain that was signed by Jennifer, her attorney, and the U.S. attorney on July 11, 2022. The following, as outlined by the Department of Justice, U.S. Attorney with the Southern District of New York, describes a small portion of the plea bargain that I took note of:

RE: (US V. Jennifer Shah – S4 19 Cr. 833 (SHS)

- *"On the understandings specified below, the Office of the United States Attorney for the Southern District of New York ("this Office") will accept a guilty plea from defendant Jennifer Shah ("the defendant") to Count One of the above-referenced Indictment. Count One charges the defendant with participating in a conspiracy to commit wire fraud in connection with the conduct of telemarketing and carries a maximum term of imprisonment of 30 years; a maximum term of supervised release of five years. In addition to the foregoing, the court must order restitution as specified below."*

- *"In consideration of the defendant's plea to the above offense, the defendant will not be further prosecuted criminally by this Office (except for criminal tax violations, if any, as to which this Office cannot, and does not, make any agreement) for participating in a conspiracy to commit wire fraud in connection with the conduct of*

> telemarketing, in violation of 18 U.S.C. §§ 1349 and 2326, as charged in Count One of the Indictment."

- "The defendant hereby admits the forfeiture allegation with respect to Count One of the Indictment and agrees to forfeit to the United States, pursuant to Title 18, United States Code, Section 982(a)(8) a sum of money equal to $6,500,000 in United States currency, representing proceeds traceable to the commission of said offense (the "Money Judgment")."

- "The defendant further agrees to make restitution in an amount ordered by the Court up to $9,500,000, pursuant to ..."

- "It is understood that the sentence to be imposed upon the defendant is determined solely by the Court. It is further understood that the Guidelines are not binding on the Court. The defendant acknowledges that her entry of a guilty plea to the charged offenses authorizes the sentencing court to impose any sentence, up to and including the statutory maximum sentence. This Office cannot, and does not, make any promise or representation as to what sentence the defendant will receive. Moreover, it is understood that the defendant will have no right to withdraw her plea of guilty should the sentence imposed by the Court be outside the Guidelines range set forth."

- "It is agreed (i) that the defendant will not file a direct appeal; nor bring a collateral challenge, including but not limited to an application under Title 28, United States Code, Section 2255 and/or Section 2241, of any sentence within or below the Stipulated Guidelines Range of 135 to 168 months' imprisonment and (ii) that the Government will not appeal any sentence within or above the Stipulated Guidelines Range."

The above is just a short excerpt. This plea agreement, including the signature page, is six pages long and is also available online. The plea agreement was followed by Exhibit A: "The Consent Preliminary Order of Forfeiture/Money Judgment" (delineation of Jennifer's payment of $6,500,000 to the government).

Reading through the plea agreement gave me some peace. Knowing that Jennifer could possibly be imprisoned for her actions was welcoming news. Shortly thereafter, I learned that the money laundering charge had been dropped, per Jennifer's plea bargain. Once I learned that her sentencing date was scheduled November 28, 2022, I entered this date on my calendar and prayed that she would receive the maximum number of years allowed by law. So, I patiently waited for that day to come, which I knew would be a long-awaited day of reconciliation for myself and the other victims.

CHAPTER EIGHT
THE LONG PAUSE

Soon after Jennifer entered her guilty plea, Special Agent Kelsey, and the assistant attorney asked me if I wanted to write a Victim Impact Statement. I quickly obliged because I knew this would give me the opportunity to express how Jennifer's con game impacted me physically, financially, and emotionally. Since I did not get the opportunity to testify and tell my story in court because of Jennifer's plea bargain, I felt that writing an impact statement would afford me that opportunity on the date of her sentencing, which was set for November 28, 2022. I began drafting my impact statement about two weeks after her plea hearing and forwarded the final draft to Special Agent Kelsey at Homeland Security Investigations on July 25, 2022. I wanted nothing more than to be in the courtroom on the day of Jennifer's sentencing, but my schedule would not permit me to travel because it was too close to the Thanksgiving holiday. Still, the fact that my voice would finally be heard through the reading of a letter was just as impactful. My letter, as presented below, laid out the ugly truth about my encounters, the losses I incurred, and the devastating effects it all had on me.

Your Honor,

I would like to thoroughly describe the effects that the criminal actions of Jennifer Shah have had on me. Not only has her actions caused financial stress for me, but I have also suffered emotional and physical stress due to her actions as well. My overall health is forever changed.

I was excited at first about beginning a new career for myself back in October of 2017. I was on the verge of retiring as a special education teacher and I was searching for another career that could supplement my small pension. I completed some job searches online and received some inquiries, but nothing materialized right away. Shortly thereafter, I received a phone call from one of Jennifer's partners about starting a successful home-based, ecommerce business. He was very convincing. He kept using the phrase, "Using other people's money to make money." It seemed promising and legitimate, so I agreed. I bought several services, including a website, which I charged to multiple credit cards. This was the biggest mistake I had ever made in my adult life because from that point on, my life began to spiral out-of-control.

I had accumulated a little over $35,000 in credit card debt by early January 2018, with no profits to show. It all felt so surreal. According to Jennifer's partners, all I would need to do is pay the minimal balances. Still, it was hard for me to grapple with the fact that I actually used my credit cards to pay for those services. Nevertheless, I worked diligently by devoting more than 10 hours a day to my business. I followed the guidelines, I took very good notes, I asked questions to gain clarity, I researched certain topics on my own, I wrote and posted several blogs on my website, and I completed all the homework that the coaches assigned to me. Still no profit. It wasn't long before I realized that I was being scammed. But it was too late because Jennifer and her partners already had my money.

Sleeping at night became increasingly difficult because I constantly worried about my financial situation. I only had a small pension. It was not enough to pay my mortgage, utilities, household expenses, and the monthly credit card payments across four different accounts. I grew dizzy at times, started sweating more than usual, and I became increasingly weaker. I worried all the time.

On February 14, 2018, the worst thing imaginable happened to me. I suffered a heart attack and had to be admitted into the hospital. The doctors stated that my heart attack was brought on by extreme stress. I had encountered Takotsubo Cardiomyopathy (a heart condition triggered by intense emotional or physical stress which causes sudden chest pain and shortness of breath), and elevated blood pressure. I had to undergo an exploratory procedure to determine if there was any damage to my heart. Thankfully, there was no damage.

Before this heart attack, I did not take prescription medication on a regular basis, just vitamins. Following my heart attack, I was placed on four different medications. I had to learn ways in which to control my stress to avoid another heart attack. So, I changed my way of thinking and began practicing calming and relaxation techniques. I refocused my attention and efforts toward my ecommerce business because I was determined to earn a profit. Again, I worked diligently every day, I continued to follow my coaches' guidelines, and I completed the homework assignments.

Then, beginning in March 2018, I was completely locked out of my own website for a few weeks. I didn't understand what was happening because my website was completely paid for. After several inquiries, I finally learned from a support team member that my website's hosting service had changed hands, and that I would soon regain access to my website once the transition was completed. Once I regained access to my website, however, the format had completely changed and all of the articles that I worked so diligently on were no longer visible on my website. The products that I had downloaded to my website for dropshipping purposes were in total disarray. I was furious! I tried repeatedly to contact the support team to resolve these problems, but the team did nothing. In June 2018, one of Jennifer's partners called and tried to sell me yet another product for $1,800 to fix all of the errors that were on my website. That was it! I refused to pay another dime! I wanted out at this point.

Beginning in July 2018, I shifted by attention and efforts toward shutting down my business and requesting refunds from all the partners, including Mastery Pro Group. It was not an easy task, however, because I kept getting referred to different people within the resolution department. Yet, I didn't give up and I kept pressing the issue, but this only led to more stress and aggravation. On August 8, 2018, I had another heart attack and was hospitalized once again. The doctors performed the same procedure that they had done before to determine if there was any damage to my heart. Fortunately, again there was no damage.

The medications that I was prescribed, however, caused side effects and had to be changed from time-to-time. To this day, I am still living with some side effects (dizziness, severe skin discoloration, light- headedness, blood pressure spikes, trembling, tiredness).

Just about every day, I live with an uneasy feeling that if I experience any other stressful situations, I will have another heart attack. Since my first heart attack, I have had my blood drawn and checked every six months followed by visits with my primary care doctor. In addition, I have had regular six-month visits with my cardiologist and an electrocardiogram (EKG) performed during each visit, or sooner. These doctor visits and procedures are ongoing. I have since been to the Urgent Care Center on two occasions, and to the Emergency Room for heart and blood pressure related issues. Last year, early 2021, my cardiologist ordered an echocardiogram which revealed that I now have a leaky heart valve. I am scheduled to have another echocardiogram later this year to determine if there are any changes.

I believe that I should receive full restitution from Jennifer Shah to cover the entire amount that I invested and lost as a result of her fraudulent activities, which was $35,290 (the minimum investment). Additionally, I should receive **twice the above amount in restitution** for my medical expenses and pain and suffering. The side effects that I am experiencing, and the emotional and financial strain that Jennifer and her partners have caused me are ongoing. Each doctor visit, medical procedure, emergency room visit, and hospital admission added up to high deductibles and co-payments which I paid out-of-pocket. I am still paying for an emergency room deductible, and I will continue to make higher co-payments for my cardiologist visits and medical procedures indefinitely. My FICO score also suffered as a result because my credit card balances were very high. Prior to starting the ecommerce business, my FICO score was 804 and by June 2018 it had fallen to 711. I am still trying to pay off one of those credit cards which has an outstanding balance of $4,900. I still have not been able to raise my FICO score above 800.

Not only should Jennifer pay restitution, she should also be given the maximum prison sentence allowed by law. I hope and pray that she has or will have genuine remorse for her actions and have plenty of time to think about her actions. She took advantage of vulnerable, elderly people. I am 60 years old now, so I may never bounce back from my medical, emotional, and financial situation caused by Jennifer and her partners. I may never be made whole again!

Respectfully,
Bridget Knight

There was nothing much more to do now but wait. My impact statement had been received by the assistant attorney and I felt like the weight of the world had been lifted from my shoulders. November couldn't get here fast enough. During the interim, I tried to keep myself busy by working on certain craft projects around my home, connecting with my family more, and meeting up with friends that I hadn't seen in a while. The busier I kept myself, the quicker time passed by. November had finally come at last! I kept checking my email for any new information or updates from Homeland Security.

Then, unexpectedly, I received an email from the United States Department of Justice, Federal Bureau of Prisons, on November 18, 2022. This would be the first of many emails. The email pertained to the criminal case of Jennifer and all her co-conspirators. The purpose of the email was to notify me about the Justice Department's Victim Notification System (VNS), because I had been identified by law enforcement as a victim during the investigation of the criminal case against Jennifer and her co-conspirators. I was directed to register with VNS, and by doing so, "It would allow me to access all notifications regarding the case, view any additional documents provided during the case, and allow me to update my personal contact information." Registration was completely optional.

Since I wanted to receive updates and view all notifications about Jennifer and her associates, I registered with the Victim Notification System without hesitation. Within a short while, I started to receive updates about Jennifer and each one of her co-conspirators. These updates included the types of charges filed against each defendant, the dates they were arrested, the upcoming dates for their sentencing, their years and/or months of incarceration, their release dates, etc.

There were many co-conspirators that I learned about; some who had already pled guilty and were currently serving time or awaiting their sentence, and others who had pending charges filed against them. I was stunned by what I learned about each defendant through the VNS.

November 28, 2022 was quickly approaching but I hadn't gotten any updates about Jennifer Shah's sentencing in particular. When I still didn't receive any news on November 28th or shortly thereafter, I concluded that Jennifer's sentencing had been postponed. It was soon confirmed through the VNS that her sentencing was rescheduled and would occur on January 6, 2023. The "long pause" had just gotten longer.

CHAPTER NINE
THE SENTENCE

Jennifer's new sentencing date was set for January 6, 2023, but she was not alone. I learned that one of her co-conspirators, J.C., would also be sentenced on this very same day. Suddenly, I became curious about J.C. and all the other co-conspirators, so again, I started to do some digging. I had plenty of questions and was hoping to find answers through the Department of Justice's Victim Notification System (VNS).

- How many co-conspirators were there altogether?
- What were their names?
- What role did each one play in the grift?
- What charges were they actually facing or are already facing?
- Did they all plead guilty?
- How many years in prison were they facing?

- How many are currently serving a prison term?
- Were any of them given probation?

There was a plethora of mind-blowing information on the Department of Justice's Victim Notification System's website, so I felt compelled to share this information. I compiled the following list of Jennifer's thirteen co-conspirators, their charges, the outcomes, and other case-related details, as provided and summarized by VNS:

Co-Conspirator #1: C.A.
- Arrest date: November 20, 2019
- Charged with one count of Attempt and Conspiracy Fraud
- Outcome: guilty
- Reason: plea
- Ordered to serve four years in prison, followed by three years of supervised released

Co-Conspirator #2: C.B.
- Arrest date: November 20, 2019
- Charged with one count of Attempt and Conspiracy Fraud
- Outcome: guilty
- Reason: plea
- Sentencing hearing date: April 26, 2023

Co-Conspirator #3: A.C.
- Custody status: Bureau of Prisons custody
- Charged with one count of Laundering of Monetary Instruments
- Charged with one count of Attempt and Conspiracy Fraud
- Outcome for each: guilty
- Reason for each: plea

- On January 6, 2023, defendant was ordered to serve six months incarceration, followed by three years of supervised release

Co-Conspirator #4: J.C.A.
- Sentencing hearing rescheduled (originally set for November 16, 2022)
- Charged with one count of Manufacture, Distribute or Dispense Controlled Substances/Possess with the Intent
- Charged with one count of Attempt and Conspiracy Fraud
- Charged with one count of Drug Abuse and Prevention of Controlled Substances – Attempt and Conspiracy
- Outcome for each: guilty
- Reason for each: plea

Co-Conspirator #5: J.C.
- Sentenced by court January 6, 2023
- Charged with one count of Attempt and Conspiracy Fraud
- Outcome: guilty
- Reason: plea
- Upon release from confinement, the defendant/inmate will be on supervised release for two years

Co-Conspirator #6: M.C.
- Sentenced by court
- Charged with one count of Attempt and Conspiracy Fraud
- Charged with one count of Tampering with a witness, victim, or an informant
- Outcomes: pending

Co-Conspirator #7: J.D.
- Sentenced by court
- In Bureau of Prisons custody

- Charged with one count of Attempt and Conspiracy Fraud
- Outcome: guilty
- Reason: plea
- The court ordered the defendant to serve two years, six months of imprisonment, followed by three years of supervised release
- Currently incarcerated; scheduled for release on March 21, 2023
- Not eligible for parole

Co-Conspirator #8: K.H.
- Arrested December 6, 2019
- Sentencing hearing: April 14, 2023
- Charged with one count of Attempt and Conspiracy Fraud
- Charged with one count of Laundering of Monetary Instruments
- Charged with one count of Manufacture, Distribute or Dispense Controlled Substances/Possess with the Intent
- Charged with one count of Fraud and Related Activity – ID Documents
- Outcome for each: guilty
- Reason for each: plea

Co-Conspirator #9: S.H.
- Arrested November 20, 2019
- Charged with one count of Fraud and Related Activity – ID Documents
- Charged with one count of Fraud – Loan and Credit Applications, etc.
- Charged with two counts of Attempt and Conspiracy Fraud
- Charged with one count of Laundering of Monetary Instruments

- Charged with one count of Using Fire/Explosive or Carrying Explosive Involving a Felony
- Charged with one count of Fraud by Wire, Radio, or Television
- Charged with one count of Fraud and Related Activity – Access Devices
- Outcome for each: guilty
- Reason for each: plea
- Sentencing hearing set for May 30, 2023

Co-Conspirator #10: D.L.
- Custody status: in Bureau of Prisons custody
- Charged with one count of Tampering with a Witness, Victim, or an Informant, which was dismissed without prejudice
- Charged with one count of Attempt and Conspiracy Fraud
- Outcome: guilty
- Reason: plea
- The court ordered the defendant to serve six years of imprisonment, followed by five years of supervised release
- Scheduled prison release date is February 21, 2027
- Not eligible for parole

Co-Conspirator #11: J.M.
- Charged with one count of Attempt and Conspiracy Fraud
- Outcome: guilty
- Reason: plea
- Sentencing hearing scheduled for June 13, 2023

Co-Conspirator #12: J.S.
- Arrest date: March 11, 2019
- Custody status: in Bureau of Prisons custody

- Charged with one count of Laundering of Monetary Instruments
- Charged with one count of Fraud and Related Activity – ID Documents
- Charged with one count of Federal Offense
- Charged with one count of Attempt and Conspiracy Fraud
- The court ordered the defendant to serve one year of imprisonment, followed by three years of supervised release; furlough approved, beginning April 7, 2023
- Scheduled release date is December 23, 2023
- Not eligible for parole

Co-Conspirator #13: S.S.
- Charged with one count of Tampering with a Witness, Victim, or an Informant
- Charged with one count of Laundering of Monetary Instruments
- Charged with one count of Attempt and Conspiracy Fraud
- Outcome for each: guilty
- Reason for each: plea
- Sentencing hearing is scheduled September 7, 2023

As anyone can plainly see, Jennifer Shah and her co-conspirators had been quite busy over the last decade, leaving a trail of destruction or ruins in their path. They ruined their victims financially. They ruined their victims mentally. They ruined their victims emotionally. They ruined their victims physically. The lives of these victims, including my own, will probably never be mended or restored to its fullest. It is more difficult for an older person to bounce back from financial devastation, for instance, than it is for a younger person. I guess this never entered the minds of the defendants, which is shameful. Not all of the above defendants were directly associated with Jennifer Shah's company, Mastery Pro Group, but according to the special agent, "They ran their own floors and knew one another, and were all doing the same thing." I continue to get regular updates about Jennifer and all her co-conspirators from the Victim Notification System.

Things were now in motion. Jennifer's sentencing hearing was held January 6, 2023, as scheduled. There was no way to listen in on the hearing, so I was at a disadvantage. Still, I was somewhat pleased with the Judge's decision. The prosecution was seeking 10 years of incarceration, but Jennifer only received six years and six months, followed by five years of supervised release. A few days after Jennifer's sentencing, I was able to locate the following court document outlining the restitution order decided by the judge on January 11, 2023.

"CONSENT ORDER OF RESTITUTION"
"UNITED STATES OF AMERICA v. JENNIFER SHAH, Defendant"

"The Defendant's conviction on Count One of the above Indictment; and all other proceedings in this case, it is hereby ORDERED that:
1. Amount of Restitution -
Jennifer Shah, the Defendant, shall pay restitution in the total amount of $6,646,251.00, pursuant to ... to the victims of the offense charged in Count One. The names and specific amounts owed to each victim are set forth in the Schedule of Victims, attached hereto. Upon advice by the United States Attorney's Office of an address of a victim, or any change of address of a victim, the Clerk of the Court is authorized to send payments to the most recent address provided by the United States Attorney's Office without further order of this Court."

- A. "Joint and Several Liability - Restitution is joint and several with the following defendant in the following case: S.S. ..."
- B. "Apportionment Among Victims - Pursuant to ..., all nonfederal victims must be paid before the United States is

paid. Restitution shall be paid to the victims identified in the Schedule of Victims, attached hereto, on a pro rata basis, whereby each payment shall be distributed proportionally to each victim based upon the amount of loss for each victim, as set forth more fully in the Schedule of Victims."

This document further delineates the "Schedule of Payments, Payment Instructions, Additional Provisions, and Restitution Liability." The above is only a brief summary. This entire document can be located online.

Although Jennifer's plea bargain orders her to make restitution to the victims in the amount specified, the restitution process would take a long time, according to the special agent. This could be worrisome for some elderly victims, especially those over the age of 70 or 80. *When will they actually receive restitution? When will they be made whole again? When will they fully recover from this and other losses they suffered? What would justice look like for them?* These victims are the ones that concern me most.

As of the writing of this book, Jennifer Shah has already begun serving her prison sentence. She was incarcerated on February 17, 2023. For Jennifer and her co-defendants to have orchestrated such an elaborate con for so many years without being detected is simply ludicrous. Con artists, however, are very clever at their game. *What really goes on in the mind of a grifter? What are the perplexing tricks of the trade? How could someone truly thwart a scam before they are hooked by the grifter?* I had more questions than answers, so I made it a mission to uncover or peel back the layers of their sick, twisted practices to try and understand their underlying motives. What I discovered was absolutely chilling. I knew I needed to share what I uncovered with other people, both victims and non-victims.

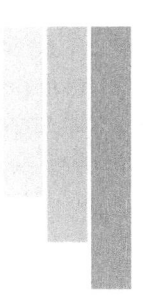

CHAPTER TEN
THE TRUTH BEHIND THE GRIFT

Swindlers, con artists, grifters, scammers, tricksters, fraudsters – it doesn't matter which term you use to describe a cheat; they basically operate from the same set of rules from the same playbook. In an article written by Ed Grabianowski in 2021, *How Con Artists Work*, the author states that, "Con artists make money through deception. They lie, cheat and fool people into thinking they've happened onto a great deal or some easy money, when THEY are the ones who'll be making the money. If that doesn't work, they will take advantage of our weaknesses – loneliness, insecurity, poor health or simple ignorance. The only thing more important to a con artist than perfecting a con is perfecting a total lack of conscience."

Grabianowski further states that, "Despite what you may think, a con artist isn't always a shady-looking character. A con artist is an expert at looking however he needs to look. If the con involves banking or investments, the con artist will wear a snappy suit. If it involves home improvement scams, he'll show up wearing well-worn clothes. Even the basic assumption that the con is a 'he' is incorrect. There are plenty of con women too."

He explains, "You might think that you can spot a con artist because he's someone you instinctively 'don't trust.' But the term con artist is short for confidence artist – they gain your confidence just long enough to get their hands on your money. They can be very charming and persuasive. A good con artist can even make you believe he or she is really an old friend you haven't seen in years."

Grabianowski goes on to explain that "Con artists do share certain characteristics, however. Even the best con can only go on for so long before people start getting suspicious. It would be impossible to catalogue every con, but con artists are inventive. While many cons are simply variations on ones that are hundreds of years old, new technologies and laws give con artists the opportunity to create original scams. Many cons tend to fall into a few general categories, however: street cons, business cons, internet cons, loan cons, and home improvement cons."

Jennifer's associates, whom I spoke with, definitely exhibited the characteristics of a con artist, as described by Grabianowski in his article. They were able to "talk a good game" and win my confidence long enough to get me to buy their products and services. They managed to hook me rather quickly. I could only surmise that Jennifer Shah exhibited the same or similar traits as her "partners-in-crime." Still, what were the reasons that drove Jennifer and her co-conspirators to do what they did? In an article published by Bence Jendruszak in 2017, *Psychology of Fraudsters 101*, the question, "What drives fraudsters to commit crimes," was answered and explained as follows:

> "The intrinsic drive to committing fraud may be explained by two simple factors of greed and dishonesty. Although, the case is not this simple, as scientists still have not been able to find precise psychological determinants that would serve as indicators in measuring the motivation for an individual to commit fraud. Monetary burdens are factors of motivation in

almost every type of fraudulent activity. This leads to the point that in several cases, building wealth may be a matter of ego for individuals. Some may consider that when getting rich is a megatrend, to go by any opportunity of becoming prosperous may be considered missing the boat. Another source of motivation may be a choice of a hectic lifestyle filled with drugs, drinking and casinos."

So, was it Jennifer's quest or desire to become rich or prosperous "by any means necessary?" Was it the lavish lifestyle that she wanted to maintain? Was she driven by greed? Was she trying to "keep up with the Joneses" by buying expensive clothing, shoes, and designer handbags that she really couldn't afford? Was she trying to impress her friends and followings? Was she trying to seek attention, or did she love the attention that she was already getting? Only Jennifer really knows.

TRICKS OF THE TRADE

There are some things about con artists or swindlers that are certain. They prey on those who are vulnerable. They have a way of catching their victims off guard, gaining trust, and "sliding in for the kill." In a 2022 Readers Digest article entitled, *12 Tricks Con Artists Use to Win Your Trust*, the author, Brandon Specktor, brilliantly describes how, "Getting conned could be as simple as a stranger knowing your name, so be careful." The 12 tricks that Specktor described are as follows:

1   **Con artists are masters of trust.**
'A con artist's only weapon is his brain,' says celebrity con man Frank Abagnale, author of the memoir *Catch Me If You Can*. So, what do Abagnale and other con artists know that you don't? For starters, con artists know how to earn the confidence of strangers in seconds flat.

2   **Con artists target the vulnerable.**

If you've ever been scam (and most of us have, in one way or another) it doesn't mean you're stupid – it only means you were vulnerable. That's because scam artists play to *emotions*, not intelligence. 'People who are going through times of extreme life change, for instance, are very vulnerable to con artists because you lose your equilibrium,' says science writer Maria Konnikova, author of *The Confidence Game; Why We Fall for it ... Every Time*. You end up more susceptible to all types of cons when you, for instance, have lost a job... [but] positive changes also make you vulnerable – you start being more credulous of good things in general.' Other easy targets? The lonely, the elderly, and the insecure (usually men) are notoriously easy targets.

3 **Con artists get you talking – a lot.**
The most successful cons hinge on desire – what can the con artist offer the victims that will make them abandon rational thought for the promise of fantasy? The best way to discover someone's desire: ASK. 'Victims don't ask a lot of questions; they answer a lot of questions,' writes a retired telemarketing scammer. 'Victims don't look for why the offer is a scam; they look for why the offer will make them money. They want you to make them feel good so they can pull the trigger.' A scammer not only needs to be a master actor but a master listener. And they have tricks for that, too. Watch out!

4 **Con artists say your name.**
'It is crazy how much more we will like someone if they remember our name, 'Konnikova says. A name creates a sense of familiarity, but it can also serve as a distraction. Professional card hustlers, for instance, might even say your name to draw your attention away from their mischievous hands.

5   **Con artists mimic your posture.**
Numerous studies show that mirroring body language increases empathy. It makes salesmen or saleswomen more likely to close deals, and it allows con artists to build subconscious bonds with their victims. Mirroring creates a feeling of familiarity and belonging, and most importantly to scammers, it breaks down mental defenses by allowing access to their victims' physical space. Be on your guard when approached or meeting face-to-face with potential con artists.

6   **Con artists show their flaws.**
Con artists tend to be great talkers. And speech can be manipulated just as effectively as body language to build a quick sense of familiarity between the scammer and victim. A good con artist will put his or her victim at ease by telling stories that reveal his or her own anxieties, faults, and desires, thereby fabricating what feels like common ground. As research shows, we are quick to trust people we see as imperfect (like ourselves).

7   **Con artists call on influential friends.**
SOCIAL PROOF, one of psychologist Robert Cialdini's six principles of persuasion, says that people are more likely to do things if they see other people doing them first; You are more likely to friend a stranger on Facebook if the two of you have mutual friends, right? But social proof is easier to fabricate than you'd think. A retired telephone scammer recalls how his company hired TV's Adam West to unwittingly help sell an internet-kiosk scam. 'I guess people see an Adam West on TV and assume the product he's selling is the real deal or else he wouldn't be selling it. But West's contract frequently states that he cannot be held responsible for the accuracy of the claims in the script ... he may know nothing about the business. He just comes in, reads the lines, and leaves.' The first day the company's

Adam West ad ran, it generated more than 10,000 phone calls.

8   **Con artists let you win at first.**
The easiest way to build up a victim's confidence is to give them a taste of reward. To that end, many scams begin by letting the victim win something – be it money, affection, social acceptance, etc. The classic three-card monte scam is a great example. The dealer draws players in by letting them correctly pick one out of three shuffled cards a few times in a row before subtly changing his shuffling method, tricking the player's brain and robbing them blind.

9   **Con artists set a ticking clock.**
The same way retailers influence shoppers to buy more with tempting 'limited time only' sales, con artists use the 'time principle' to persuade their victims to act quickly before rational thoughts and self-control can kick in.

10 **Con artists start small.**
There are scams that start by asking the victim for progressively larger favors, starting small. Konnikova calls this the 'foot in the door' technique. 'Clearly, if I've said yes to you in the past, that means that you're worth it,' she says, 'otherwise it would have been very stupid of me to say yes before.' In one online dating story, a woman was seduced by a dating site scammer who asked her for progressively larger money transfers – first $8,000, then $10,000, then $15,000 – with the promise that it would help him clear customs and permit a long-term relationship together. She ended up giving him more than $300,000 before the scam was exposed.

11 **Con artists dress the part.**
As stated earlier in this chapter, a con artist is an expert at 'looking the part.' One retired con man admits, 'This was

Lesson No. 1. Swindling is really acting, and you play a character who will help you appear legitimate, confident, and successful... even if you're not.' At age 17, Frank Abagnale famously bought a pilot's uniform so he could pass fake checks at any hotel, bank, or business in the country without question, because 'pilots are men to be admired, trusted, and respected. And you don't expect an airline pilot to be a local resident. Or a check swindler,' he explained.

12. **Con artists rely on your embarrassment.**
Konnikova says, 'It is crazy how often you have people who, even when you present them with evidence that they've been the victim of a scam, refuse to believe it. We often don't want to let other people know, because we are embarrassed.' Such was the case when early con man Victor Lustig convinced a Paris metal dealer that he was selling the Eiffel Tower for scrap to the highest bidder. Lustig conned the man out of a $70,000 bribe in exchange for rights to demolish the tower and take possession of 7,000 tons of metal. Of course, this was all a lie. But the dealer never reported the scam; he was too embarrassed.

Finally, Con Artists love this phrase.
You and I are going to make a lot of money together. If someone says this to you, ask yourself, what's in it for him or her? If you can't find an answer, run. Or simply hang up the phone.

PULLING IT ALL TOGETHER

After reading both Grabianowski's and Specktor's articles, they gave me clarity and confirmation. Both articles revealed just how the minds of swindlers work and how easy it is to become a victim of their grift. The grift is real. When I was reading these articles, I tried to relate it to my own experience with Jennifer Shah's associates. I thought back to each time I purchased products and services from them and how all the signs were visible, but I ignored them at first. Jennifer's associates were all cunning and brilliant at their game, all using the same playbook to gain my trust and convince me to buy their products and services without thinking it through thoroughly.

I remembered the language that David and the others used, and the key phrase, "Creating wealth by using other people's money." This phrase was repeated over and over again. I trusted what he and his associates were selling because talking to each one was like talking to someone of high esteem. They were believable.

They quickly targeted my vulnerability when I expressed my desire to retire early from the school district and my desire to supplement my pension income with a home-based business. This was going to be a life-changing event for me, so they played on my emotions.

I remembered how much we actually talked. We talked for what seemed like hours initially; triggering me to agree and make the purchases for the website setup, the LLC Entity setup, the Corporate Credit package, and the Tax Preparation Program. These products and services were sold to me in rapid succession in a matter of minutes. I didn't have time to think rationally because I was too busy talking and signing the purchase agreements.

Thinking back, I remembered how David and the rest always used my first name when addressing me, as if we were pals and had known each other for many, many years. I felt at ease talking with them and trusted everything they were selling. As stated earlier, *"A name creates a sense of familiarity, but it can also serve as a distraction."* They cleverly distracted me long enough to get me to sign each purchase agreement without giving it a second thought.

The tricks that con artists use to reveal their flaws, as stated earlier, is spot on. Again, *"They put their victims at ease by telling stories that reveal their own anxieties, faults, and desires, thereby fabricating what feels like common ground."* I distinctly remember David and the others using this trick by talking about their own personal backgrounds and triumphs that mimicked my own personal challenges and my desire to become successful. They were only telling me what I wanted to hear. They wanted me to think that they were once in the same boat as myself, yet they were eventually able to create wealth through their ecommerce businesses. I told myself, "If they were able to do it, so could I."

"When con artists call on influential friends to sell their products, they do this a number of ways, thereby providing "SOCIAL PROOF." I recall the time when I was instructed to look at several videos online, via webmarketservices.com. These videos portrayed stories of other peoples' successes after they invested in the same ecommerce business. Realistically, the individuals portrayed in those videos could have been actors, simply reading from a script. They were only saying what they were instructed to say. Yet, I was ignorant of that fact.

Again, the "easiest way to build up a victim's confidence is to give them a taste of reward," so it's no mistake that "con artists let you win at first." To recall, I purchased a professional, custom-built, well-designed website at a discounted price. The regular price was $12,600, but Jennifer's associate offered it to me for $9,800. This was the reward! A few months later, Web Market Services shut me out of my website without any warning. They then wanted me to pay $1,800 to fix the errors and restore my website to its original state. Another clear example was the one-year membership plan that I purchased from Doba.com for dropshipping at the special price of $2,500. The regular price was $4,000 and this price would have been charged automatically to my credit card each year. Con artists build you up, only to let you down.

Applying pressure by using a "ticking clock" to persuade victims to buy, buy, buy quickly is a trick that all of Jennifer Shah's associates used masterfully. For me, this was evident by the special pricing of the website design and setup, the reduced pricing for the fourteen coaching sessions, the discount for the dropshipping membership plan with Doba.com, etc. It was almost as if I needed to buy these products and services as soon as they were introduced, to fulfill the next objective that would become essential to finally making big money.

The above tactic pretty much ties in with the trick for how a con artist "starts off small at first," and then makes progressively more requests that will drain your pocketbook over time. As I stated earlier, the purchase of one product or service led to another, then another, then another… until I accumulated about $35,000 in credit card debt. There seemed to be no end in sight. I hate to imagine how much more debt I would have accumulated had I not ended my business with Web Market Services, Prime Corporate Services, and Mastery Pro Group.

I communicated with Jennifer's associates entirely by telephone, so I had no idea as to how they were dressed. Had I been able to FaceTime them or if they had been featured in YouTube videos, I imagine they would have been dressed in their "Sunday best." As stated previously, con artists "have to dress the part." If they intend to sell products or services, claiming that they will make you wealthy, then they themselves must exude wealth or success by looking their very best. Even when talking to Jennifer's associates by telephone, I imagined how they were dressed. I pictured all of them wearing expensive, tailor-made suits and being very well-groomed.

I can truly relate to the fact that con artists see their "marks" as being too embarrassed to believe that they've been conned or too embarrassed to even report the con to authorities. Some people will always live in denial. When swindlers aren't reported, they move on to the next unsuspecting soul, crafting and enhancing their skills more and more each time. For me, I was able to admit to myself that I had been conned, but because I was too embarrassed, I didn't tell any family or friends about the con until 2021, nearly four years later. On the other hand, I did come very close to filing a consumer complaint against Web Market Services, Prime Corporate Services, and Mastery Pro Group. However, because I received a small refund from Mastery Pro Group, I decided not to move forward because of the agreement that I signed. I truly regret that decision.

There is no denying that con artists love the phrase, "You and I are going to make a lot of money together." I had heard this phase used by swindlers in the distant past multiple times, and fortunately, I didn't fall prey to their con. I was younger and wiser back then; before encountering Jennifer's associates. I actually thought I could easily spot a con, but Jennifer's associates didn't make it easy for me. They were so cunning. To reiterate, the phrase they loved to use was, "Creating wealth by using other people's money." That phrase was the hook. Once I finally recognized the con, they already had my money. Once a con gets a hold of your money, you may never, ever get it all back, or get any of it back.

If you've been conned once, does it mean that it will be easier for you to spot or avoid the next con? Will you fall prey to another con? It's important to equip yourself with the facts about con artists and how they operate to avoid getting swept up in future cons. If you feel or suspect that you have been conned, report it immediately. Throw nothing away; "keep a paper trail." Keep all the email messages, text messages, telephone logs, session notes, personal notes, dates and times, full names, purchase agreements, etc. Arm yourself with evidence to present to authorities or lawyers when that time comes. Be diligent. Do the opposite of what a con artist expects you to do.

CONCLUSION

There are indeed legitimate home-based businesses out there. Unfortunately, there are some really bad players who make it difficult for those wanting to invest in an honest work-at-home business. Unfortunately, I was dealt a bad hand. Jennifer Shah and her associates were the epitome of bad players. They were grifters, probably driven by greed. Together, they swindled nearly five thousand unsuspecting souls, mainly the elderly, by proclaiming that they could create wealth by establishing an ecommerce business, which turned out to be worthless. It was all a lie.

Jennifer and her associates got richer, and her victims got just the opposite. Yet, they continued to sell their useless products and services, time and time again to satisfy their greed. They did a great job of crafting and covering up their scam for the most part, but even the best con artist will one day be exposed. With the brilliant work of Homeland Security Investigations and other law officials and authorities, Jennifer's illegal telemarketing empire was shattered and brought to its knees. Although their empire has been ended, it may not necessarily be the end for their five thousand victims – including myself.

I am inclined to believe that what happened to me is representative of what happened to the other five thousand victims; falling prey to the same or similar tricks of the trade and selling tactics employed by Jennifer Shah's associates. We, the victims, are not stupid people. We are smart and resilient. I earned my master's degree in special education in 1990, and my master's in general School Administration in 1997, with a keen focus on climbing the ladder of success. I know that there are other well-educated victims of Jennifer Shah's who are, perhaps, still aiming for great achievement or success. I know that I am not alone.

We, the victims, were trusting and willing to take chances. We were eager to build wealth or simply supplement our income by working from home. We believed that our investments and hard work would pay off. We didn't recognize the con and, sadly, this caused Jennifer and her associates to prey on us. We were victimized over and over again, each time we purchased one of Jennifer Shah's products and services.

I still have some nagging questions running through my mind, however. "How do we actually recover from it all? How do we move forward? What does the future hold for us or look like for us? Moving forward, how do we protect ourselves from other scam artists? Can we honestly trust our instincts?" These are tough questions that I don't have all the answers to, but there are a few ways that we can better equip ourselves in the future to avoid the next scam.

Below, I have included some valuable information that may be helpful, not only for victims, but for anyone who's serious about operating a home-based business that's legitimate. Some of this information have already been covered in previous chapters, but it's worth repeating because it's presented somewhat differently here because of how it correlates with home-based businesses.

To begin with, there are several ways to avoid becoming a victim of a home business scam. You just need to take notice of the warning signs. Con artists are slick, so you have to be quick. In a post that I discovered on HindeSights.com, entitled *How to Avoid Home Business Scams and Tricks,* the author writes about "some things to look out for when starting a new business."

The author explains that "If there is a claim that you will get rich overnight or gain unbelievable wealth with almost NO effort, this is a red flag. If it seems unbelievable, it is! Check with the Better Business Bureau and with the Attorney General's office in the state where you live. Read user reviews from reputable websites and check consumer reporting publications and websites. With all the information available online, there is no excuse for being taken advantage of." It's important to do your due diligence. The author further explains that,

> Hard work will always be an ingredient for a successful business, so never believe it when someone tells you that a business will practically run itself. It will not. The effort you put in will be

directly proportional to the results that come out of it. So many people fall into the trap of thinking there is a quick fix for money problems. Nothing will ever replace demanding work, dedication, and a vision for the future.

Fictional testimonials are a dead giveaway of scams. If you read testimonials that are glowing and sound like they are coming straight form a script – they are. It is quite likely that these people have been paid to say the things they are saying, or they may even be total fabrications. Ask for direct contact numbers for anyone claiming to vouch for the business opportunity and ask them specific questions that they would only be able to answer if they were genuine business owners who had used the products, for instance, and sold it to clients.

Be very wary of anyone who asks for a large upfront investment of cash, especially if it is nonrefundable. No refunds, no way! Ask questions about 'free trial' periods, making sure to read the fine print. These offers will often require you to give a credit card upfront, which will be charged the entire fee for buying into the business. Then if you have issues or do not want to continue, you can request a refund of this fee. You can bet that it will not be easy at all to ever get this refund. If they are genuinely offering a free trial, then it should be FREE, with on upfront cost whatsoever.

High pressure sales tactics are another sign of home business scams. Never give into high-pressure tactics and immediately cut off communications with anyone who tries to reel you in this way. It is indicative of desperation and an attempt to get you signed up before you can realize the flaws and inherent dangers in the program or the product. They may also be trying to get you to 'sign on the dotted line' before reading the small print and the required commitment.

Lastly, always take as much time as you need to think it over and to determine whether it is the right business for you. If the product is of as high quality as claimed, they are not hurting for your business. There should be no urgency for you to close the deal. If you do sign, you generally have 72 hours to cancel the contract so do your due diligence.

Don't let fear or embarrassment hold you back. Report the scam immediately. Persistence pays off. The bottom line is, "You can avoid home business scams and build a successful business in the process." I only wish that I had been knowledgeable of the "12 tricks of the trade," and had the above information in my arsenal when I received that very first phone call from Jennifer's associate. I could have avoided the $35,000 credit card debt. I could have avoided the two heart attacks that I suffered due to the stress of it all. I could have avoided the rapid drop in my FICO score. I could have avoided the feelings of shame and embarrassment. I could have avoided the losses. Simply put, I could have avoided the "Jennifer Shahs" of the world.

If I had only known the truth when I was faced with the truth back in 2017, my financial situation would be completely different today. I would not have been vulnerable and fallen prey to a second scam – the Belize scam. So, yes – a second scam occurred less than two years after the Jennifer Shah scam. This was the main reason why I couldn't build my beautiful house in Belize. The Belize scam has many layers and many moving parts. Just as in the case with Jennifer, the fraudster targeted elderly victims, mostly over the age of 55. Unlike Jennifer's case, this scam has not been extinguished yet. I like to think of it as Jennifer's telemarketing scam *on steroids*. But that's another story to tell in my next book, at a later time.

I wish I hadn't been so naïve back then. I wish I had been stronger and shrewder. But you know what people say – "hindsight is 20/20." The only thing that I can do now is learn from my past mistakes and be more diligent in the future. I am armed with knowledge now. I now know the signs and the tricks of the trade. It is my hope that others will recognize the signs and evaluate their situation carefully before getting caught up in a "web of deception" and losing their hard-earned money to a swindler. Recuperating quickly from a scam may be impossible, but avoiding a scam altogether could be quite possible. Don't become a victim of a con. Recognize the warning signs and take action. Your pocketbook will thank you later.

ACKNOWLEDGEMENTS

First and foremost, I am grateful to God for the wonderful daily blessings he has bestowed upon me. He has given me patience, hope, clarity, and strength to make it through the tough times. He has surrounded me with family and friends who care and support me unconditionally; always looking out for me and going out of their way to bless me with kind words and actions. He gives me courage to be unafraid and to share my stories with others, no matter how painful or embarrassing. I am grateful for all that He does.

I am also grateful for my editor, Marina W., who is passionate about her craft and in helping authors to achieve their goals and taking their writings to the next level. Her passion for writing and editing was shown in the way she communicated honestly, in the way she applied constructive criticism, and in the professional manner in which she collaborated to ensure a sound, outstanding product. She is an amazing editor.

Lastly, I am grateful for my close family and friends, *listed below*, who were instrumental in helping me to select a design for the cover of my book. Some offered honest, constructive feedback. Others offered amazing, new ideas. Above all, they all showed compassion and excitement. It was also through their encouragement and support that this book was even made possible. I am forever indebted to them. I am honored to have them in my life.

Kathryn Anderson
Mark A. Anderson
Sylvia Carmonds
Theresa A. Chaney
Melani Hutchins
Donn Kelly
Lillian Kelly
Sidney and Debra Kelly
Bruce Kemp

Theresa L. Raglen
Guy and Danielle Vezina Regniere
Janay Salmon
William Salmon
Gail Thornton

Printed in Great Britain
by Amazon